Disaster Among Us

I0170155

Copyright © 2015 by   Cynthia Moore
Inner Harmony Books
P.O. Box 16783
Sugar Land, TX 77496

Editing, Cover Layout and Design by Kitty Y. Williams

Front Cover Background Image (the cabin in the woods) courtesy of: © Can Stock Photo Inc/lenm. Additional modified illustrations of the characters and back cover image are courtesy of the public domain.

ISBN-13: 978-0-9789961-4-7 Paperback
ISBN-10: 0-9789961-4-3

Printed in the United States of America: First Printing

To order additional copies of this book, visit:
www.DisasterAmongUs.com

For more books by Author Cynthia D. Moore, check out:
www.InnerHarmonyBooks.com

1

About the Author

This is the third book release for Houston area Author Cynthia D. Moore. **Soul Say Yes** was published in 2014, followed by the 2nd edition of her original book, **ABCs of Relationships: Emotional Survival Games**, the same year. She holds a Master of Science Degree in Counseling Psychology, is a Licensed Professional Counselor in Texas and has worked with various populations in the mental health field that include:

- Clinical Director and Coordinator - Residential Treatment - Children, Adolescent, Teen/Young Adults

- Inpatient Hospitalization - Adults, Children and Adolescents

- Partial Hospitalization - Dual Diagnosed Adults with both severe Mental Illness and Chemical Dependency

- Intensive Outpatient Program - Mental Health Adult Intensive Groups

- Lead Clinician - Assertive Community Treatment - Psychosocial

- Rehabilitation Mental Health Outpatient Adult Population

- Practice Manager of two Mental Health Outpatient Clinics

- Behavioral Care Advocate - Utilization Management

- Private Practice

Acknowledgements

I am so thankful for the heavenly inspiration of God and his host of Angels that surrounded me through the writing of 'Disaster Among Us'. Without their loving nudging, persistent encouragement and guidance, the story would not have come together as well as it did.

I want to thank my sisters, my niece Danielle and especially my great niece Janelle and nephew John for their feedback. A big thank you goes out to Music Producer Kenny "Dubb" Williams whose song "Stomp the Ground" inspired a few of the profound messages in this book. As always, thanks to all of my children for continuing to believe in and support me through each publication. To my Mother and Father who have always promoted my worth and cheered my endeavors, I truly appreciate you. Finally, I want to personally thank YOU! That's right, you there reading my book at this very moment. Believe it or not, I wrote this for you!

From the Desk of *Ms. Cynthia*

A Word from the Editor

I too thank you for reading and encourage you to share 'Disaster Among Us' with everyone you know, even strangers you don't know. In editing Cynthia's book, I learned a few things and you will too. We need you all to understand that no matter how crazy the world and people around us may become, no matter how many times disaster may strike, no matter how often our circumstances may seem completely unfair, there is ALWAYS hope. Hope for deliverance during challenging times, hope that our needs will be recognized and we will not be forgotten, hope that someone will show us they genuinely care when we are at our most vulnerable. Do keep the faith.

There is something even better than hope and faith: ACTION. It is ok to stand up for yourself and your rights as a beautiful citizen of this universe. It is even better to be proactive in lending a helping hand to those in more need than ourselves, with or without a reward, even if we're hurting too. Be that loyal friend someone can depend on through good times and bad. Never stay stagnant in a pit of negativity. Don't stand by and allow others to bully those who may not have the strength or resources to defend themselves. Whatever the situation, it is totally ok to make a difference. In fact, be the difference by your existence in itself. Someone is always watching.

Love You Always, *Kitty W.*

About Disaster Among Us

Having held positions as Clinical Director and Coordinator for state and privately funded residential treatment centers, Cynthia's observations of children without parents were at times absolutely heartbreaking. From those experiences, she has always wanted to help raise awareness about the many obstacles they face in the absence of their families; the goal being to help protect the rights of our most vulnerable citizens.

Disaster Among Us demonstrates character building through a group of female critters who find themselves trying to survive in a yard together, despite their conflicting differences. Those differences bring unexpected challenges which require them to muster up courage, confidence and gain power over their insecurities and fears of each other, or else meet their demise.

Much of the story takes place around a shack and its oblivious owners. The Critters eventually find themselves on a very important mission beyond the yard, in the wilds of the woods, that forces them outside of their normal everyday functioning. Ultimately, they each realize their value to the group while maximizing their unique abilities and inner strengths for the greater good.

Editor's Note: 'Disaster Among Us' is a timeless story for mature readers of All Ages and is not specifically intended to be a Children's book, in spite of the cover.

TABLE OF CONTENTS

About the Author

Acknowledgements

About Disaster Among Us

CHAPTER 1

CHAPTER 2

CHAPTER 3

CHAPTER 4

CHAPTER 5

CHAPTER 6

CHAPTER 7

CHAPTER 8

CHAPTER 9

CHAPTER 1
Mama's Drama

Once upon a time, there was a Wasp, a Bird, a Cat, a Rat, a Dog and an Opossum whom all lived outside of a shack. Now mind you they were not pets, but random critters that migrated to the yard. As far as The Critters were concerned, the owners had intruded on their territory when they built the shack.

One day one of the owners of the shack, Mrs. Jacks, heard a loud noise outside as if a fight was happening. She quickly peeped through the window and saw a bird flying fast, furious and squawking at a wasp in the corner of the porch; it was building a mud nest right next to her hatchlings. The bird was not having it and made such a fuss that the wasp flew off.

Mommy Nancy, the Bird, sat for a moment and once she thought all was clear, flew off as well.

Meanwhile Pauli, the Cat who had been taking shade lying underneath a bush, roared with laughter and began taunting Queenie, the Wasp, for trying to build the nest right next to her enemy. "What is wrong with you?" she shouted. "You know it is in a bird's nature to have you for dinner. Are you going blind these days?" Both critters chuckled.

Queenie buzzed, "You are supposed to beckon me and chase that squawk off."

"Sorry Queenie, I got sidetracked when I suddenly caught a strong whiff of my supper. Well the coast is clear now so hurry up and do what you need to do," replied Pauli.

Queenie thanked her companion, gently reminded her not to let it happen again and resumed building the nest.

Pauli tried her best to stay focused but soon became distracted again with Suzie the Rat and purred, "Oh well, I've got my own family to worry about." She then took off to chase after her dinner.

CHAPTER 2
Mrs. Jacks to the Rescue

Well it was not long before Mrs. Jacks heard another loud noise outside, then went to the window and saw the bird flying and squawking louder than ever. The bird was trying to get the wasp away from her hatchlings and at the same time avoid becoming the cat's dinner.

Pauli was confused as ever as she tried to catch Suzie and divert Mommy Nancy away from Queenie simultaneously.

This time Mrs. Jacks thought perhaps she should attempt to break up the fight. As she was contemplating going out, suddenly her big dog known in the yard by the other critters as 'Titanic', appeared from the corner of the house and began chasing the cat. It was pure war and every critter for themselves.

Queenie was fighting with Mommy Nancy, Pauli was chasing Suzie while at the same time trying to save her life from Titanic, and Suzie was just happy for the diversion. It was a hot mess all in one small afternoon.

Mrs. Jacks said, "I'm going outside to break this up right now!"

But Mr. Jacks said, "No. Let it be because those critters are doing exactly what is in their nature."

She replied, "But Henry, they are going to hurt each other and one of them may get killed!"

To which her husband responded, "It will not be the first time."

11

Mrs. Jacks then snapped, "I cannot stand by and do nothing!"

"Ok Penelope, I cannot stop you. Go in at your own risk but make sure you have protection," he answered.

So she gathered some critter spray, a broom and headed out to break up the fights.

Mr. Jacks chuckled, "I thought you said one of the critters may get killed?"

His wife looked at him, "What do you mean?"

He laughed so loud, "It looks as if you are joining the fight with all of your weapons. Some things are better left alone and unless those critters come inside, they're on their own."

Penelope decided she had a bone in the fight and explained that the grandbabies were coming over and she did not want the wasp to sting them, nor the bird to run them off of the porch or for them to get hurt from the dog chasing the cat.

Henry sighed, "I thought you were a neutral party but I guess you have no other choice."

Mrs. Jacks stood pondering for a few seconds but as the noise became louder, rushed outside to break up the fight.

The moment she opened the shack's door, the fight suddenly subsided. Titanic ran back around the corner; Pauli stopped chasing the bird and rat; Queenie and Mommy Nancy flew off in opposite directions; and Suzie disappeared into the field. Mrs. Jacks was relieved that she did not have to use her weapons, while her mate stood by and just shook his head.

CHAPTER 3
Disaster in the Shack

Penelope went back into the shack and began preparing her own supper; low and behold a critter had gotten inside. She screamed and shouted, "Oh my goodness, oh my goodness!"

Henry ran into the kitchen and when he saw what made her scream, he roared with laughter and asked, "Where are your critter spray and broom now?"

Screaming even louder she fussed, "Just get it, get it! Oh my goodness, if it is not one thing it is another."

"That's right; this is the world we live in. Did you think this shack was sitting in the garden of paradise? This is where you wanted to retire right?" Mr. Jacks pulled himself together and said, "I guess I will join the fight." Grabbing a shoe, he chased and caught the intruding critter then removed it from the shack. Walking away, he looked back and saw flies gathering together for their unexpected and fortunate supper.

Later that evening while the couple sat having tea, they heard their dog barking loudly as she chased an opossum who was searching for food in the yard. Mr. Jacks resigned, "Survival of the fittest is no fun as everyone has a predator. I guess we all have a bone in this fight."

CHAPTER 4
The Day After the Fight

By the next morning, all of the critters were tired and frustrated that they had not accomplished their goals the prior day. Queenie did not finish building her mud nest and Mommy Nancy could not tend to her birdies because the Jacks had moved them after the fight. Pauli the cat never got her meal. Suzie the rat was so depressed that she did not make it back to her pups and instead had to sit quietly underneath the shack all night waiting for the coast to clear of Pauli, Mommy Nancy and Tamera the opossum. Of course Tamera did not get her meal because Titanic chased her off before disappearing back around the corner.

Suzie was so exhausted from trying to save her life all day that she squealed, "We are all trying to survive out here, so can we come to a meeting of the minds?"

Pauli roared with laughter and shouted, "Yes! Let's agree you are my next meal."

Mommy Nancy squawked at Pauli for being such a bully and said, "Too bad you were not quick enough, or you would have gulped her down already."

Queenie, keeping one eye on her predator, sneered and asked Suzie, "How do you propose that we come to a meeting of the minds when Nancy can devour us both, Pauli can devour you, and Titanic can devour Pauli and Tamera?"

Mommy Nancy jumped in, "It is no secret that we are all vulnerable to each other with our instinctual urges one way or the other and have the ability to devour. Perhaps we can simply start with setting boundaries

15

and respecting each other's space, which is what started this whole fight anyway. Now I have to relocate my babies. Is it not clear that we are all trying to survive out here in the same yard?"

"Boundaries," Queenie retorted, "how about a meeting of the minds on sharing?"

Pauli shouted, "I most definitely agree because that big canine Titanic thinks she owns the yard and poor Tamera can't find her dinner in peace."

Suddenly a loud rustling noise from around the corner growled out, "Did someone call for the canine?"

Pauli crept back under the bush and said, "No," then purred, "mind your own business."

Titanic woofed, "You are my business. By the way, I know I'm big and robust but my name is Charlene, not Titanic."

"Sure, whatever you say big pooch," mewed Pauli.

"I need to get back to my pups," fussed Suzie, "so can we figure this out because we're all out here trying to make it and take care of our families."

Pauli teased, "I am hungry and the more I hear you squealing, the more my palette waters for you. If it was not for Titanic, I mean Charlene, I would have gobbled you up by now."

"You just may get your wish because I am going to shrivel away from hunger soon if I can't get a meal," squeaked Suzie.

Charlene growled, "Oh, stop all the fuss. We're all endangered to some degree. Instead of terrorizing each other with pending doom, let's figure out how we can all help each other and coexist."

"You look like you are surviving just fine," Pauli whimpered.

Charlene snarled, "Perhaps we need to focus on jealousy Queenie."

Queenie whizzed through the air and swirled rapidly around in a circle to get everyone's attention. Then in a hoarse raspy tone she told Pauli, "I empathize with you about Titanic, but perhaps she has a point."

"I told you my name is Charlene, not Titanic."

Queenie shrieked out, "Titanic we have been calling you that for a long time now, it is going to take a moment, so chill out. I am trying to agree with you here that we all possess unique skills that can help each other survive. So let's help ourselves, by helping each other." Suddenly the shack's door opened and all of the critters retreated to safety.

CHAPTER 5
Charlene Reaches Out to Suzie

Charlene who had retired under the shack tried to nudge Suzie out of her hiding place by asking her what she thought about the impromptu meeting of the minds.

Suzie squeaked, "It doesn't matter anymore, because I'm getting weaker and weaker."

"Here Suzie, take my bowl. I'd hate to see you croak over there. Where are you from anyway? I have never seen you around here."

The rat shared that she and her family ran from a burning field they had lived in after a fire broke out in the woods.

"Well," said the dog, "you're not any safer in this yard especially with Mommy Nancy, Pauli and Tamera hanging around. One of the three will get you for sure."

Suzie shivered, "If they do not, the owners certainly will. They got my cousin yesterday when she snuck into the shack to find food. I watched Mommy Nancy scoop her up from the hovering flies. That is why I'm hiding."

"We definitely have quite a bit of negotiating to do, because staying alive is bigger than us all," concurred Charlene.

"There is no way we can all come together and agree on existing in this one yard," challenged the skeptical rat.

"With that kind of doubt you will always find yourself running and hiding, and for that I will call you 'Doubting Suzie'."

"No, no," Suzie defended, "I'm just trying to keep it real because when you see your flesh and blood eaten by those air scourges... What do you expect me to say?"

Still chomping on her bone the pooch replied, "I expect you to say, 'Thank you' for the meal that you did not have a few moments ago and perk up with a little bit of optimism."

"Ok Charlene, you're right. I am just overwhelmed right now. Thank you."

"You are welcome and thank you for calling me Charlene. Only my enemies call me Titanic."

Queenie suddenly swirled from around the corner buzzing over and over, "Five minutes until the 'Disaster Among Us Meeting of the Minds'. The coast is now clear."

Suzie snapped, "I am not going out there."

"Ok Doubting Suzie, keep hiding and stay underneath the shack. You and your family will not be included in any decisions we make. Though let me remind you, this was your 'great idea', so the least you could do is show up."

"Well as you can see Charlene, my ideas so far have gotten me nothing but trouble. My cousin is gone and I am not with my family because of my 'great idea' to come to this yard looking for food.

"Go ahead and sit there in that little dark hole and feel sorry for yourself, or you can follow through now that you have all of our attention," bayed Charlene.

Disaster Among Us

Pauli, lying lazily nearby on her back purred out, "Tell ole Suzie she is safe; I will not eat her. I've had my meal for the day."

"You better not, or you're going to have to deal with me. Now leave us alone before I have you for dinner," Charlene cautioned.

"That sounds terrorizing," snarled the cat.

CHAPTER 6
The Critters' First Official Meeting of the Minds

Suzie cautiously eased her way from her dark hole and merged onto the outer yard.

Charlene, seeing her hesitation woofed, "Come on my little friend, let's go!"

Queenie circulated around to get all of the critters' attention again and buzzed, "'The Disaster Among Us Meeting of the Minds' will open with a platform discussing each of our strengths that we contribute to the yard. We will re-visit this every time we get off task as a reminder about the importance of our coming together."

"That sounds like a good place to start and how about you open with your strength, miss busy bee?" Mommy Nancy squawked.

Queenie flew into a vertical position and softly announced, "It is my honor to do so. As you all know darlings, you have enjoyed the beautiful fruit trees, vegetable and flower gardens, and the wonderful sweet golden honey in the yard. Well I work very closely with one of the most prominent and hardest working families here, the honeybees, who pollinate all of the crops and plants. My family and I are in charge of keeping away intruding pests that may want to harm those plants. Without our protection, neither you nor the owners of the shack would be able to enjoy these glorious benefits."

Pauli licked her mitts and purred, "Thank you Dauber family, I love that yummy honey. By the way, how does your family do that? It is such a mystery."

"No, it's no mystery darling, but is unique to honeybees. See, we all have our unique contributions," declared Queenie. As a fact, that is exactly what I was doing when the fight started between me and Mommy Nancy. I was building my nest to catch insects."

Nancy chimed in and chirruped, "Well seeing that I am of the wild and not a domesticated fowl, I too enjoy that sweet honey nectar; but building your mud nest right next to my hatchlings puts them in danger of your enemies. Furthermore, what if the Jacks burn down my nest trying to rid their shack of your mud nest?"

"Nancy, no matter where we set up our nests, there is a risk of danger everywhere. That is the nature of where we live."

"But if I can minimize that risk I will!" snapped the bird.

"Queenie and Nancy please stay on task," barked Charlene. "And by the way Nancy, what is your contribution?"

"I thought it was obvious," Nancy peeped. "I help control insects in the yard too. I also twitter beautiful sounds as I take care of my family. The Jacks have made mention many times of my beautiful singing. Let's not forget that all of you but Queenie aspire to have my skill of flying. So I have a far better vantage lookout for the yard than ole Pauli."

"Oh, stop bragging." Pauli droned in.

Charlene barked loudly, "Focus Pauli! What is your contribution?"

The cat rolled over onto her back and purred, "Just look at how cute and cuddly I am. I contribute companionship. Mr. and Mrs. Jacks just love me!"

Charlene howled and yapped, "Used to love you."

"Now Titanic that was not necessary; I know you two have your differences but it does not hurt to show a little compassion for Pauli's dilemma with the owners. After all, Pauli has been a very good friend to me," Queenie butted in.

"Okay, you are right Queenie; but just a friendly reminder, I said my name is Charlene. Perhaps respect should be added to the agenda, instead of making excuses like 'This is what we have always called you'."

"Well, what is your contribution Ms. Charlene?"

Proudly wagging her tail with great importance, she responded, "I contribute protection in the yard from uninvited predators as well and that makes Penelope and Henry feel safe."

"Hear ye, hear ye, shady, shady, shady Titanic!" shouted Pauli. "So we are now on a first name basis with the owners?"

"Oh Pauli, your jealousy is showing again. We all know what happened to you and the Jacks, so calm down. I don't have to throw you any shade since you're already laying in it. This is my last reminder by the way, my name is Charlene."

"Go ahead and threaten me," snorted the cat.

Charlene rose up but then withdrew, "Never mind. Keep calling me 'Titanic', because 'Charlene' is too classy for you anyway. If you had any class you would have been able to stay inside with the Jacks and not get replaced by their new young feline, Onyx. So go right on with your antagonizing."

Queenie furiously hovered over the squabbling critters with her stinger out and reprimanded them both for getting off the subject at hand. She reminded them of the meeting's agenda.

Charlene hollered, "Oh Queenie, that old stinger does not scare me; save the intimidation for your insects."

"Sure you're right. But you know Pauli doesn't mean you any harm, even if she is being inappropriate."

"Well she needs to mind her manners with me," expressed the dog.

Pauli feeling slighted put her head down on both paws and murmured, "Is this meeting over yet?"

Mommy Nancy curiously inquired, "I want to know what happened to Pauli and the shack owners. Pauli, why did you get kicked out?"

"Hold on. Let's focus please because it is getting dark and Suzie needs to find her family, but first we need her input." Queenie then turned to Suzie and asked her contribution.

"Well honestly," revealed Suzie, "after listening to everyone else, I just don't know what I bring to the yard. I am always on the run and hiding just to save my life. I would love to have security, a companion, hum harmonious tunes and have time to munch on insects and honey too. If I am your meal and always on the run, how can I contribute? It is just too much," she sniveled before bursting out into huge tears.

"Oh please Suzie, get off of your pity party," meowed the hungry cat. She then mumbled under her breath, "I don't know why I agreed to this meeting anyway. I ought to pounce over there and grab you for a late snack; then you would have a reason to feel sorry for yourself."

Disaster Among Us

Queenie, partly with a smirk on her face commented, "Pauli, I can hear you and that's not nice." She then turned to all of the critters and announced, "Well since Suzie is unable to identify her purpose in the yard, we will just have to help her figure it out. As she just summed up, so far our duties include keeping it free of pests, enjoying beautiful tones, providing companionship and security. We also learned that we each bring similar value but in our own unique ways, all seemingly just as important to our shared space here. This yard would not have its beautiful characteristics without our combined efforts. Now we just need Suzie and our friend of the night Tamera's contributions. We will entrust Charlene with the task of getting that for us."

"That opossum is not going to allow me near her," woofed Charlene.

"Well," bossed Queenie, "it looks like you have some making up to do. Your work is cut out, so do the best you can."

Charlene perked up her ears, "I have to go. My owner Henry is calling for me."

"Ok, we will meet again tomorrow after supper. We don't want any hungry critters in the meeting. Also, hopefully Suzie will be ready to recognize and share her importance to the group.

As the critters began to depart, Charlene called to Suzie, "Come with me my little friend. You can stay with me on the back porch for the evening and I'll help you find your family tomorrow." Suzie exhaustedly agreed.

CHAPTER 7
Meeting After the Meeting

Still brooding over Charlene bashing her, Pauli eased over to Queenie and purred, "I thought you would always have my back."

"You have to stop being so catty, picking fights and expecting others not to retaliate against you or not to hold you accountable for all that extra purring."

"I'm sure you are right, but Titanic really hurt my feelings when she mentioned Onyx. You see I have known Onyx's family very well and shortly after they took him from his family, his twin brother passed away and now he's all alone."

"Pauli I understand, but you and I have a relationship. I know you're harmless, but the other critters don't know your intentions and are bothered by your sarcasms. We both know Titanic has a low tolerance for foolishness and will retaliate when pushed in a corner. She is also going to take up for anyone she thinks is being attacked. So your taunting Suzie is luring in Titanic to rip you apart, one way or the other. I suspect that she has her own problems that someday may gush out and when they do, she will need our support; however for now she is clearly on the defense. After all, this is how you and I became friends. Remember the first time when we met on the porch? You were no different than Suzie and were very defensive like Titanic. You were hurt, confused and lost out here in the wild after the Jacks put you out to fend for yourself. You had no companion and you were a companion to no one. I watched you for days just sitting there lost on the porch looking as hopeless as Suzie. Even now you only venture to the edge of the yard and not into the woods like other wild critters. So when I see you taunting

26

the rat, I wonder if you have forgotten your own plight of separation from your family. I suspect that Titanic's intentions were not to hurt you, but just to give you a tough reminder of your reality in order for you to show a little patience and empathy toward Suzie."

"Thank you Queenie, I see your point. I just hate to see Suzie sulking, depressed and not fighting for her survival; so my chase is to motivate her."

"I hear you Pauli," buzzed Queenie. "I suppose the venture of the chase is very exciting for you but all critters are not motivated the same way and most are simply just trying to survive from day to day."

"Queenie, you have given me much to think about. With that said, I bid you goodnight."

CHAPTER 8
Suzie Searches for Her Pups

The next day all of the critters went about their daily routines and Charlene set out with Suzie to find her family. They hurriedly brushed through the fields. As they combed through the bushes, Charlene beckoned for Suzie to slow down because she was starting to pant.

"Hurry Charlene, please! I think I see my uncle at the edge of the field!" She squealed very loudly to get his attention and they were very happy to see each other. Her uncle was slightly startled at the dog's size and asked Suzie about her huge friend. "Uncle, no worries. This is my friend Charlene and she looks out for me."

"She is a mighty big friend," he replied.

"Yes indeed," she laughed.

Suzie and her uncle chatted about the disastrous fire that caused their family to scurry from the field. After a few minutes of sharing their plights to save their lives, she decided it was time to give him the bad news about her cousin, Deidra.

He wept that he had suspected she did not survive the fire.

His niece revealed, "No uncle. She survived the fire then snuck into a shack for food but did not escape before the owners caught her." Suzie then sobbed, "Uncle why, why, why are things this way!!! Our family has roamed this meadow for many generations and Deidra and I were very close since we were young." She then looked around for her pups and did not see them. Even louder she wailed, "Where are my pups?"

"Suzie, your babies are fine and they survived the fire. Russell, my canine friend, saw them at the north end of the field along with your cousin's pups and their aunt. You know your aunt is very clever, just like Deidra was, and she will look out for all of them."

CHAPTER 9
Suzie Gets a Lesson on Reality

"Suzie it is not time to be depressed," asserted her uncle. "It is time to adapt to your new environment and figure out how you are going to make it in spite of this recent disaster, and in the absence of your running mate. I know you miss Deidra hon, but you know the Norway pack's history. At one time we lived completely in the wild but the humans continued to develop the land for their dwellings and use, so we have had no choice but to adapt to new ways of functioning in order to sustain ourselves. I too am very sad about the blaze, but we are survivors in spite of all our challenges in the wild. Although the fire is a disaster of sorts, it is also forcing us to evolve to another way of survival. That is why our kind of critters have managed to stay around for such a long time. We must be grateful because there are many others who did not escape this event or even just being in the wilderness. They are not as quick and as small as we are to navigate through it all.

"It all just seems so unfair that the owners of the shack would not spare your daughter. Oh, I miss her and it is just too much!! Why can't we all just live and let live uncle?"

"Oh Suzie, my little doe," he squealed, "as much as I loved my little Deidra and understand that she was simply trying to survive, unfortunately she violated the humans' space which brought her to an early demise. I too miss her," expressed her uncle. "My love, you are very skilled. Please go on and do not live your existence in naïveté or carelessness. Your pups will need to know that they are designed to adapt to a variety of disruptive, disastrous events. With that said, they must allow their skills to evolve where they do not cross the boundaries

30

of others. After all, we are not cuddly creatures like some other critters that the humans allow into their homes. Now cheer up my sweetheart. Winter is coming and we will all meet up again near the Leander family's barn; then we'll know at that time who survived the fire and vote on a new leader who will take us to a new field to live in.

Charlene, who had been resting but listening in the background, came forward and asked her new pal to come back to the yard with her until the winter season.

At first Suzie hesitated, but her uncle encouraged her to take the canine up on the offer. He reminded his niece that her babies were doing exactly what she needs to be doing and that is surviving. In addition, going back with Charlene would also improve her own survival skills, which could help her become the Norway family's next leader.

As the dog and rat turned to head back toward the yard, Suzie asked Charlene to give her one more moment with her uncle. She then shared with him the critters' meeting of the minds discussion and asked him about their family's contribution to a yard.

He shouted, "Suzie, were you not listening to me? Have confidence! The answer is right before your eyes and in your existence."

CHAPTER 10
Suzie and Charlene Bond

As Suzie quickly advanced back to the yard with her companion, she couldn't help but to think about what her uncle had shared regarding her family's existence alone being a contribution. She tried to chit chat about it with Charlene, but being so preoccupied with her own losses, had not even noticed how hard her friend was working to keep up. When Charlene did not respond, Suzie suddenly realized that she was limping and panting then suggested they stop for a rest under a shade tree. She then inquired of Charlene what had happened to her leg.

"Suzie, it's a long story and no use in mulling over it now. It is all in the past anyway," she yelped.

"But it looks to me like it is in your present because we had to stop and rest," rebutted Suzie. "I shared my stuff with you, so it is your turn now."

"Ok, if you really want to know; but don't say I did not try to avoid telling you... I ended up in the Jacks' yard after escaping from my last owner while at a canine show. I hurt my leg trying to break free from my kennel after realizing the latch was not secured. My owner had been beating me to get me to do tricks for the shows; it was just awful. His wife would hear him yelling and kicking me but never tried to stop him. I finally realized that she could not stop him because he was doing the same thing to her. The worst part of all Suzie, is that I left my pups there." Charlene held her head down as if in disbelief of her own decision. She went on to share, "I tried to take them with me but could not release the latch on their kennel. I heard the owner's and another voice and hid in the woods, waiting for them to leave so I could go back and get my babies. When they realized I was missing, they immediately left to search for me.

While they were out trying to find me, I returned to the kennel and realized my pups were gone. I was going to give up and just wait for the owner to come back but when I heard his voice again, and the tone in which he called me, I just could not take it anymore and fled." Charlene fought back her tears and whimpered, "I think of my family every day and hope they are okay. My only hope is that he sold them to new owners. So Suzie there you have it. You are not the only one without your loved ones or being forced to start over. I told you it is not something to mull over because thinking about it only makes me very sad and angry."

"Oh Charlene, I am so sorry. Looks like disaster is just everywhere and in this case there is no meeting of the minds. Do the Jacks treat you ok?" asked Suzie.

"Oh yes! It took me a while to feel safe with them, but they are real fine people. I learned that not all humans are corrupt."

"Charlene you are so strong!" squealed Suzie.

"Well I have to be and so do you," she woofed. "We cannot let obstacles over take us."

"Maybe someday you and your pups will reconnect," Suzie said optimistically.

"Maybe. However for now let's get back to the yard before some of my wild canine cousins, the wolves, begin to hound me."

As the pair made their way back through the woods, Charlene shared another story where she had fought off one of those cousins while living with her previous owners. She yammered on that she was only doing what was expected which was to keep wolves away from their chicken coop. The wolves never forgave her and even attempted to attack her in a pack; as a result, she stays as far away from that group as possible.

Charlene and Suzie finally arrived back at the yard just in time to hear Henry calling for her; she ran hastily towards him.

"Oh girl, there you are! Where have you been? I have looked all over for you," said Mr. Jacks. He patted his furbaby on the head and motioned for her to come get supper.

Charlene quietly shared her supper with Suzie on the enclosed back porch of the shack.

CHAPTER 11
The Critters' Second Official Meeting of the Minds

After supper, all of the critters met at the edge of the yard next to a pond and along a line of tall bushy trees. Queenie frenziedly circled around everyone, loudly giggled and then eagerly urged "Let's get this meeting started!"

"What are you in such a frenzy about?" woofed Charlene. "Have you been chewing on rotten fruit again?"

"Well, as a matter of fact, yes I have! You know summer is ending and I have been very busy producing males and new queens for next year. I am aging out and as you all know winter is coming, so my time is short."

Pauli asked, "Do we have to talk about that now?"

"Actually, there is no better time than now because shortly I will have to introduce you to a new queen. With that said, let us pick up with Suzie's contribution."

Suzie admitted, "I need a little help please."

"Alright," buzzed Queenie. "All critters have worth, so what do we think is Suzie's value?"

"I will start," Pauli purred. "Suzie you can help by keeping me up to date on how my cousin Onyx is doing in the shack."

"How do you propose I do so?" squeaked the rat.

"Well you are small enough to sneak in for me," answered the cat.

Charlene immediately interjected, "How very selfish of you to ask Suzie to risk her life for you! That is not a contribution for the yard."

Still pondering over her purpose, Suzie told Queenie she needed a little more time.

"Here, let me help you out my friend," offered Charlene. "I wasn't being nosey, but I overheard your uncle's conversation with you about your family's ability to adapt and survive more than any other critters; but they've had to do so by adjusting to new environments."

"What does that have to do with the yard? That is clearly about her family," scoffed Pauli.

Charlene turned to bark at the insensitive feline when Mommy Nancy squawked, "I get it, I get it!" and all of a suddenly, she shrieked so loudly that all of the critters took off fleeing in different directions.

CHAPTER 12
Meeting Interrupted

Unfortunately for Charlene, because of all the confusion, she fled toward the woods and right into a pack of wolves. Suddenly the other critters heard loud howling and growling, then a huge rumble.

Suzie screamed, "Oh no, oh no, help her, help her!!!"

All of the critters moved towards her and asked "What is it, what is it?"

"It's Charlene, please help her!" pleaded Suzie.

Pauli queried, "Charlene?"

"Yes! Charlene... Titanic... Please help! Her wild and ferocious cousins, the wolves, are attacking her," Suzie cried. "They probably followed her scent from our trip into the woods today. Please, her leg is already wounded from her old owner's abuse. She needs us!"

"Ok, calm down," demanded Queenie. "Mommy Nancy and I will create a diversion and you and Pauli must go quickly to get Mr. Jacks."

As strategized, the wasp and bird flew over quickly to distract the wild beasts.

Pauli purred, "Let's go. You will need to get the Jacks' attention."

"Ok," Suzie agreed. They raced back to the shack and Pauli ran onto the front porch. Suzie snuck inside through an opening she noticed the day before while hiding under the shack. She glanced around and saw Henry and Penelope sitting having their evening tea. "Here I go," whispered the rat, "this is for you Charlene," as she quickly grazed by Mrs. Jacks' foot and dashed underneath the couch.

Not surprisingly Mrs. Jacks screamed, "There is another one! Onyx, get it! Oh please, get it!"

Mr. Jacks got up but could not find the stealth rodent.

Suzie, feeling very nervous about her friend Charlene, hastily ran to the shack's front door before darting back under the couch.

He swiftly opened the door and Suzie knew she had to do what she had to do, running as quickly as she could towards Pauli, with Onyx fast on her tail.

Henry looked up, saw Pauli and realized that she did not chase after Suzie, but ran towards Onyx instead. He sensed that something was wrong by the way Onyx quickly followed Pauli. He then heard a very loud noise and realized that Charlene was missing.

He yelled, "Where is Charlene, Pauli?"

Pauli and Onyx had already run off towards the woods so Mr. Jacks grabbed his shotgun and followed them.

Suzie followed also but stayed as far back from him as possible.

Mr. Jacks then noticed the pack of wild wolves attacking something, so he fired his shotgun into the air. The wolves took off and that is when he saw Charlene appearing all torn to pieces. He ran to his companion, lifted her up and said, "I better get you some help girl or you are not going to make it through the night; plus I suspect those wolves will come back for you to ensure you won't."

Suzie squirmed knowing she could not go with them and was on her own for now. As she followed closely, she decided to hover by the hole underneath the shack.

The other exhausted critters dispersed for the evening as well.

By the time Henry reached the shack, his grandson Bobby had arrived with his mother Melissa, the Jacks' daughter-in-law, who had come over to join them for tea. When Bobby saw that the dog had been badly hurt, he rushed over to her and asked his grandfather what had happened.

When he learned the heartbreaking details, he cried "Papa, papa, you have to pray for her. Please papa, please pray that she doesn't die."

"Son, I suspect it may be too late for all of that; it looks as if Charlene is going to need a miracle," responded Mr. Jacks.

"Momma, No! Please call Pastor Jones to come pray. He said miracles are for doubters. Momma, please!" Bobby screamed.

"Son that's right, but not everything is fixable," said Melissa. "What I do not understand is why you are falling out in disbelief and doubt. Right now you're acting very pessimistic about Charlene getting better."

"Momma no..." sobbed Bobby.

"Yes you are," Mr. Jacks chimed in. "If I've ever seen a doubter, I see one now," he roared with laughter.

"Papa, it is not funny."

"Yes it is," teased Mr. Jacks. "If your behavior is not doubt, then tell me what message you're sending if it's not lack of confidence regarding Charlene getting better."

As Bobby took his shirt and dried his tears, he wishfully proclaimed, "Ok, she is going to get better."

"We are almost at the Veterinarian now and will soon see if Doctor Vale can help her," announced Mr. Jacks.

The family arrived safely to the clinic just as Dr. Vale was locking up. "It would not have been a normal day if I had closed on time. How can I help you folks?"

"Well doc," Henry shared, "Charlene was just attacked by wolves."

"I am not surprised," the Vet revealed. "We have had two other attacks in the area just this week."

"Really? I did not see any posting of such incidents, or I would have kept a closer watch on her."

"Well you have to get out more Mr. Jacks. I put a posting out the day of the first incident. Let's see how bad the damage is."

Dr. Vale whispered, "Bobby, I have confidence that you can help her. Grab my bags son and let's go."

The Doctor took Charlene in for an assessment and after a while returned to the waiting area. Leaning down to the young boy she said, "Thank you young man for your confidence. In spite of the heavy bleeding from her neck and head, there is no internal damage other than a broken leg." She then turned to Henry and informed him that Charlene also had an old broken bone injury that attempted to mend itself, but did not and was the cause of her limp. "I will need to break and recast this one as well for proper healing. Charlene will need to stay overnight for observation," affirmed Dr. Vale who then sent the family home.

Disaster Among Us

Later that evening after her procedure, Charlene remembered the high pitched buzzing and shrieking sounds of Queenie and Mommy Nancy during the attack. While she was able to gather that they helped distract the wolves, she was still somewhat puzzled as to how Mr. Jacks knew where to find her. Her gut told her that those unusual diverse new critter friends had a role in saving her life. Although faint, she remembered seeing them all there at the same time when her owner rescued her and could hardly wait to thank them.

CHAPTER 13
Charlene Copes with Her Trauma

Charlene tried her best to rest that night but could not. Although Dr. Vale had cleaned and wrapped the wounds from her head and neck trauma, she still felt the pain which reminded her that she could have easily been destroyed by the pack of angry relatives. Lying in recovery feeling restless, she wondered why they did not finish her off before Mr. Jacks sounded off his gun. She thought at first perhaps they were trying to taunt her, but was relieved to now know that they had not targeted her. The injured canine was nervous all night as she realized the shack did not have any security around it. Charlene also worried about the Jacks, because she now knew the wolves could still come back and she just didn't have the strength to fight them. She half-heartedly regretted going into the woods with Suzie that day because they had obviously picked up on her scent.

While trying to settle in for the night, she heard Dr. Vale helping another critter to do the same. There was a familiar little whimper that almost sounded like moaning. She soon realized that it was coming from another canine and heard the Vet reassure her not to worry because she was going to make sure the pooch got a good home. After the Doctor left, Charlene tried again to go to sleep but the nearby whimpering was all too familiar and made her feel really sad. She could not help but to wonder if her neighbor had been abused and wanted to get up and peep in, but knew she could not. Eventually she fell asleep.

CHAPTER 14
Charlene Gets the Most Amazing Surprise

Early the next morning, Charlene was awakened by Dr. Vale, who had come in to check on her. She could tell by the tone of her voice that she was going to be okay. Then Mr. Jacks and Bobby called out for her, "Doc, where is my girl? How is she doing?"

"Charlene!" shouted Bobby.

"It appears she is just fine and ready for you to take her home," Dr. Vale answered. Charlene was so happy to see them as she wagged her tail and barked excitedly. Mr. Jacks chuckled and picked her up.

By this time, the Doctor picked up the other pup Bliss and started walking towards the front of the clinic. Suddenly the canine leapt from her arms and headed straight for Charlene, who immediately recognized her from their old kennel club. They yapped and yammered so loudly, that the other dogs in the clinic began barking very loud as well.

Mr. Jacks and the Veterinarian could hardly hear themselves talk as they watched the two acting like old friends.

Bliss revealed to Charlene that she was there because she had fiercely attacked her owner after he kicked her several times during training. She now feared being put down and whimpered, "Oh Charlene, I know you do not promote attacking humans, but it was just too much. I do not know how you took it as long as you did. I am an old pooch and would rather have freedom in the wild or be put down than to stay with an abuser."

Charlene snuggled her and whispered, "Oh honey, I do understand. That is why I ran to the wild; you know we had plans to run for a long time. I

43

am so sorry I left you guys behind, but honestly Bliss, I have no regrets other than missing my pups. I did not plan to run on the day I left, but when the opportunity came, I knew there was no choice because my owner was not going to stop." Then she went on about her attack by the wolves and her fear that they may return.

"Don't worry Charlene. I can tell you have a good owner now." Bliss then disclosed that she had seen her friend's puppies at a training camp for an upcoming dog show. The new owners seemed very nice and were so gentle with them. She also shared how big they had grown.

Charlene was so relieved and happy to hear that her babies were safe because she had worried so much about them.

CHAPTER 15
Bliss Faces Her Abuser

Suddenly the clinic door opened and in walked Bliss' owner. Bliss wanted to run but realized she could not and that it was time to face her abuser. She braced herself as his voice and footsteps came closer and closer. Finally, she heard the Veterinarian quickly go over and inform him that a report had been made regarding Bliss' injuries and he could not take her.

"Then I want her put down for good!" he screamed. "That old pooch attacked me without cause and she will hurt someone else."

"I am not so sure about that," Dr. Vale challenged, "which is the reason why I filed an animal cruelty report with the police and am now involving animal protection services. I've put down many animals that have attacked other humans and I knew I had no choice but to do so; however in this case, I suspect your dog was provoked."

"I am going to sue you!" he screamed while storming out.

Dr. Vale stuck to her guns and said, "Do as you like, but you will not get this one back, not today anyway." Bliss was so pleased that she sat down at the Doctor's feet.

"So what are you going to do with her?" Mr. Jacks asked.

"Well I will need to secure her a foster home until the investigation is completed," replied Dr. Vale.

"Let me know if you need any help with her in the meantime, because from what it looked like, those wolves brought a couple of old friends back together again. It's amazing the things that can come out of a disaster. I tell you Doc, just when you think life is at the worst end, there is always a twist or turn unexpectedly in the road; you just have to stay on that road to get the surprises."

The Doctor then asked Mr. Jacks how long he'd had Charlene. He told her it'd been about a year now. He found her wandering along the road one evening and for some reason just felt the need to take her in.

"I do not know this for sure," said Dr. Vale, "but I suspect she may have wandered off from her owner. That old broken bone is very similar to those of other patients I've treated from a nearby kennel club."

Henry looked at Charlene and said, "Well that would explain the limp and why she was not too trusting when I found her on the roadside. Please keep me in mind for Bliss' foster care and I will talk with my wife to make sure she is okay with it."

Mr. Jacks returned to the shack and discussed bringing another canine into their home.

Mrs. Jacks who was standing over the kitchen island rolling dough to make a pizza for Bobby shouted, "No way!"

Her grandson and husband tried to talk her into it by explaining how the two dogs appeared to be old friends.

Penelope said she would check with The Bookers who lived in the shack next door; this way Charlene and Bliss could visit with each other. Henry reluctantly settled with this since he really wanted the two together.

CHAPTER 16
Suzie Recognizes Her Contribution

Charlene was still somewhat nervous about returning to the Jacks' shack, but was happy to be back home. She had to muster up every bit of courage, settle down and get back to the routine around the shack; after all, this was her territory and she could not let those wolves think it was theirs. Throughout the day while trying her best to rest, Bobby was all over his beloved companion and she loved every minute of it. The attention he gave felt so good, given the abusive environment she had come from.

As the sun set in, Charlene was still struggling to relax and could not help but to think about everything Bliss had shared about her pups; she longed to see them again, however was glad they were okay. The Jacks turned in for the night, but even the darkness outside could not bring relief to the restless pooch.

Suddenly, while lying on her blanket near the cupboard, she heard a tiny squeal, pricked up her ears and looked around though did not see anything nor anyone. She wondered if the Jacks were moving about, but could hear loud snoring sounds coming from the bedroom. Bobby was sound asleep in his room as well and Onyx was in the living room.

Again Charlene heard a squeal, but this time realized it was calling her name. A small shadow to the left, near the kitchen cupboard, turned out to be Suzie who was shaking with fear.

Charlene was so happy to see her and whispered, "How did you get in here? You better be careful or you'll end up like your cousin. If Bobby does not get you, Onyx will for sure."

"I know. I came in through the hole behind that cupboard because I wanted to see how you were doing," squealed Suzie.

"Actually I am glad you're here," whispered Charlene, "because I cannot sleep. I can't figure out why those wolves did not slaughter me."

"Oh Charlene, that is just the trauma talking. I am so glad you are ok and we were able to save you."

"What do you mean Suzie?"

Suzie explained how the critters came together and saved Charlene from the wolves. When asked if Pauli helped she answered, "Yes! She is the one that came up with the idea for us to go get Mr. Jacks."

The dog was so humbled by this revelation and whispered, "Thanks my friend." She then slid her bone over to Suzie who devoured all of the meat surrounding it. Next she dragged her blanket to cover the hole by the cupboard and said her hero could rest in the shack for the evening, but would need to leave before daybreak because Onyx is very swift and would catch her. Although Suzie was nervous, she felt very safe with her friend.

The Jacks rose up early the next morning right before daylight and saw Charlene fast asleep near the stove and cupboard. "Thank goodness that critter got in or Henry may not have been able to save you," said Mrs. Jacks. "I am so glad you are ok girl."

Suzie was hiding behind the cupboard and could hear the cat sniffing around it, but couldn't leave yet because she was waiting for the opossum to leave the yard. In the meantime, she kept mulling over in her mind about her role in helping the dog; she had risked her own life to save her friend's life. As she sat shaking, hoping not to get caught by the Jacks nor eaten by Onyx or Tamera, Suzie reflected on how she worked as a team with Pauli and didn't hesitate to come into the shack to get Mr. Jacks' attention to save Charlene.

She felt so proud to have successfully brought together a group of critters who did not appear to have a common goal; first for the meeting of the minds and secondly, for the rescue mission. She realized that in spite of her fears of the other critters as well as humans, she had responded very well during this disastrous event. Everyone worked toward the common goal of saving Charlene, which was their first big accomplishment as a team.

Suzie could hardly wait for their next meeting of the minds to share her contribution. She now understood what her uncle meant when he said their family members were survivors in spite of their challenges in the wild. She also realized her own strength was in the ability to rise above the circumstances during catastrophic times and do whatever it took to overcome them. Roosters crowing nearby interrupted her thoughts and she knew it was safe to go back outside. Charlene remained inside to heal and play with little Bobby who would not let her rest.

CHAPTER 17
Charlene and Suzie Continue to Bond

Over the next few nights, Charlene continued to bond with Suzie while she recovered. They both shared their pasts; sometimes they were just outright silly trying to keep quiet so that the Jacks, and especially Onyx, would not hear them. Suzie was beginning to feel like her old self again, yet with an invigorating and renewed twist. She felt uplifted and had much greater confidence as if she had shifted into a new zone. Meanwhile, her partner Charlene's legs were getting stronger.

Late one night while chattering away, the pair suddenly heard loud clanging and scratching noises; they laughed hard as they reminisced on the familiar sound of Tamera roaming through the night to take care of her family. "That opossum is so loud," yapped Charlene.

"Yes, yes!" Suzie squealed. "We used to hear her family seeking food when my family and I were out in the woods before the fire; we made sure to stay far away from them." Then Charlene and Suzie heard the loud clanging noise again and realized it was getting closer, seemingly trying to get their attention.

The rat perked up on her hind legs and became very nervous. Suddenly Tamera growled, "Suzie, calm down. If I wanted to eat you, I would have done so a long time ago; I've known about your hiding place since day one. Besides, Charlene would not spare me. I am pretty docile; if you do not bother me, I will not bother you. I am only here in repayment to Mommy Nancy who has so kindly shared her bird seeds with me; she asked me before daybreak yesterday to inform you all that our next meeting of the minds is in two days."

50

The Critters Finally Meet Again
Two days later, the critters slowly started gathering together in the backyard of the shack while the Jacks took a late afternoon nap. Charlene, still feeling somewhat reluctant to merge into the yard, sat on the steps next to the porch. Queenie buzzed and circled several times in and out of the gathering as if preparing for a grand entrance. Pauli laid near the bush in a very serious and sad mood. Suzie felt confident but still very mindful that the critters could devour her in an instant. Mommy Nancy opened the meeting by suddenly swooping down right into the middle of the group and began whistling a beautiful melody. She then chirped out the lyrics and told them whenever they hear the birds whistling this melody, it will be in honor of the critters bringing their differences together for one cause:

> "Our differences are greater as one
> And our oneness is boundless in spite of our differences.
> The wolves that tried to devour
> Only struck a compassionate chord of courage and harmony
> That strengthened our confidence and drove us into one accord.
> Now that we have conquered our fear of each other
> Not even the night or wolves shall ever separate us
> From such a sweet bond."

"Oh Nancy, that is so beautiful!" Suzie exclaimed. "I am honored that we brought our differences together to help save our friend Charlene. In spite of the horrendous circumstance and contrary to our first meeting, I learned that I really am a great contributor. I truly surprised myself with the tenacity that arose inside of me to save a critter of a different kind,

51

one whom I had just met; but she had been so loving towards me, that I had no choice but to rise to the occasion.

Queenie abruptly swirled around and hummed, "I also feel privileged to have had the opportunity to participate in rescuing Charlene. It has completely changed my status within my family, which gives me great honor as I depart this winter. As you all know, my time is short because the season is changing in the next couple of months. A new queen must take over and I will leave you for good. Knowing that I have contributed beyond my own kind makes me feel just absolutely awesome, more than what I can describe. I am now looked upon as a legend among the other wasps in the Dauber family for my recent participation in helping to save Charlene. When you hear their rhapsody buzzing, that will be my huge home going celebration, so please do not be sad for me."

Mommy Nancy screeched, "So dramatic but well hummed, my once mischievous competitor and now accomplice against the wolves; I would have never thought to see the day that we commune together in such space of agreement, but we do."

Pauli moaned, "Queenie, please do not leave me. You are my only friend."

"Hold on. Only in this shell will I be absent from you; as Mommy Nancy's melody goes, 'not even the night shall separate us'. You have been a friend to me as well, especially when my own family questioned my use of the fruit tree; as if I, the Queen, would misuse my pollination powers. You and I are bonded forever my dear friend. I am looking forward to finally being free forever from the wilderness, the wolves and returning to the glorious garden of peace where we will see each other again someday. So cheer up Pauli. I expect you to follow the flight of the wasps as my family sends me off with great honors when the season changes, for I am the first of my kind to bond with other critters for a good cause. In the next meeting I will introduce to you all a new queen, Lady Love, who is young and full of stings; you better be nice to her too or she will sting you!" They all shrilled with laughter.

"Oh Queenie, we are going to miss you and all of your dramatics," giggled Suzie.

Pauli hid her face and muttered, "Well, I have met Lady Love already and do not like her."

"That is not nice," Mommy Nancy chastised. "Besides, you have to give her a chance."

"I will give any critter a chance. But I know what I know and when the feeling is not right, there is something off somewhere," Pauli retorted.

"Wow," Suzie mumbled to Charlene. "Pauli is a hot mess. We are out here talking about gratitude, losses and moving forward and she is just being mean."

"No," Charlene whispered back. "Pauli is having a hard time because Queenie is leaving. I imagine taking it out on the new queen is the way she has learned to express herself. Remember, our pal there does not deal with losses very well, especially after the Jacks kicked her out. Queenie is the only friend she had after that loss."

Charlene then sat up and thanked Mommy Nancy for the melody as well as all of the critters for saving her. She yammered on that without their quick reactions, the wolves would have killed her undoubtedly.

Pauli hummed, "It was the right thing to do, Charlene."

"I will forever be grateful to all of you and look forward to more amazing harmonization of our differences," she replied.

Charlene Introduces a New Critter to the Group
Suddenly a primped white dog walked across the backyard as if she was in a kennel club show. Pauli abruptly sat up and loudly yowled, "Look at that pooch!"

Charlene barked wildly and Mommy Nancy shrieked loudly over the shack, getting the canine's attention.

Startled by all of the noise, the stranger abruptly stopped, looked over and saw Charlene sitting on the porch. She confidently high stepped right over and in a coarse mellow tone greeted the group, "Hello there."

Pauli hollered, "Where are you going all fancy there, girl?"

To which she responded, "There's nothing wrong with a pooch getting groomed up every now and then, is it?"

"Nope. But I've never seen one as dolled up as yourself," Pauli snickered. The cat looked over at Charlene, not realizing the two knew each other, and hoped she too would make a mockery at her appearance.

In a raspy tone, the new pooch on the block saluted, "Well hello there, Miss Charlene. How are you doing today?"

"Hey Lady Bliss. If I could, I would bounce right over there to rumble and tumble with you," she acknowledged.

"I know you would, you old pooch. How you feeling there?"

"Well, I am almost ready to return to the yard. Looks like you got a home at the shack next door," Charlene observed.

"I sure did, thanks to your owners the Jacks. They introduced me to your neighbors the Bookers. So what are you critters doing out here?"

"We're having a meeting of the minds," replied Charlene. "Do not mind my friend Pauli here. She doesn't mean any harm with her 'paw-in-mouth' disease; it takes her a minute to get used to new critters." Charlene then introduced her best friend Suzie and the others.

"Hey there Ms. Pauli," chatted Bliss. "I figured you meant no harm. I like when my owners primp and pamper me all up; it makes me feel real good, as long as they don't take it too far. Some of them do not seem to understand that we actually have feelings about how we are groomed hon."

Pauli purred, "It sure would be nice if all critters were treated the same by the humans. What do you think?"

"Some humans are nice and some just aren't. It depends on which one you get," Bliss pointed out. "I have had quite a few owners, both good and bad; but the ones I have now have been very pleasant. I sure hope they keep me as I am treated lovely in their care. Besides all of that, I have got to be honest... You all sure are an odd bunch hanging out together."

"That we are," barked Charlene. "But this odd group came together and saved me from those ferocious wolves that I told you about."

"Well, I sure thank you all for saving my friend here," she replied.

55

CHAPTER 18
The Critters Get a Visitor

Suddenly a bunch of leaves began twirling, chiming and quickly rose up right in the midst of the critters before they knew it. A voice said, "Your eyes do not deceive you. What you see is what you see."

"But wait," buzzed Queenie, "are you here for me already?"

"No. Your departure is between you and your creator. I am the character of Courage. The Moral Fiber Characters heard you all commending yourselves for your initiative and bravery in saving Charlene. However, uplifting yourselves with the characters of Courage and Confidence is not just supporting and inspiring each other; it is an elevation to a higher level of consciousness. This means you have overcome one fear of the wilderness and are ready to conquer another. Eventually you will arrive at the garden of peace where you will have no more fears to overcome. With that said, I do not come alone." In a loud boisterous voice Courage shouted, "Confidence, are you there?"

"Yes! (Cough, cough). Yes. Do you always have to make such theatrical and intense entrances? You know I am sensitive to all of that dust; it's all over me now. So dramatic!"

"All of my entrances are breathtaking honey," declared Courage.

"Well hello there everyone, please excuse my appearance. I am the character of Confidence. My very dusty associate here will accompany me as I direct you on your next assignment."

"Next assignment," Pauli inquired. "What assignment?"

"Well, I was just going to tell you about that before Confidence arrived," Courage answered. "Because of your great courage to save Charlene, the Moral Fiber Characters have found this group of critters worthy and are in need of your help for a very important assignment in the human community where corruption is taking place. You may decline and can continue on as you were with your self-adulation of each other; but the internal reward will not be as fulfilling as it would if you take this challenge. Should you accept, the bond that you will experience with each other at the end will far surpass the one you have now."

"Yes, yes," Confidence joined in. "It would be nice to see you all obtain such an alliance; that is, if you are able to complete the mission." She then roared with laughter as if to taunt them.

"Why would you taunt them like that? It does not boost their confidence," Courage uttered.

"Confidence booster? Are you kidding me? That I do not do," she replied. "Holding self-confidence in the highest regard? Now that I do, because out of all the spirits of character to obtain, it is the most difficult one for any creature to reach. One thing about having confidence is that most creatures have gotten the concept of my character all wrong; they think I am something that comes and goes, which is far from the truth. Many are under the impression that I am something they say to themselves over and over, or how well they look, or how well they have done. Some even believe I am the number of things they have accomplished. This is why they are forever stuck in one conscious level, always in search of me when they are confronted with new challenges versus approaching new confrontations with a foundation of me already intact. Once I am with you, I am always with you. It is simply a matter of intact moral fibers."

"Well spoken my friend and with so much passion! I could not have said it better myself and this is why Confidence is here with me today," Courage applauded. "As you know, you can all stay at your current level of consciousness with the courage you obtained by saving Charlene. However, without understanding the true meaning of "confidence", you will not maintain my character. Let me clarify. The characters of confidence and courage soar together and must be mastered from your higher self; meaning, you have to work from beyond the things you know already and sometimes even beyond your own kind."

"That is if you really want it," Confidence chimed in. "It cannot be given or taken away. You must realize your own unique abilities for it. Otherwise you will forever live in fear, will always feel intimidated by other beings and most of all, you will always observe other creatures doing exactly what it is that you want to do in life."

"This is why we are here, to make sure that no longer happens," Courage concurred. "So let us move forward to the assignment."

The Critters Get a New Assignment
"As Confidence has indicated," Courage continued, "this assignment will require four moral fibers that must be utilized throughout its completion. To use them, you will have to operate within your superior intelligence because you have to involve the shack's owners and other humans as well. Therefore, you will have the moral fibers as guides with you at all times, being objective reminders to keep you on task until this is over."

"Well, as long as we can get it done before the season changes. What is it already?" Queenie impatiently asked.

58

The Crime

"Of course, of course," replied Confidence. "As I mentioned earlier, there is corruption taking place in the human community. A fire broke out in the woods this past Spring and you all have the precise skills that are needed where the actual immorality is occurring. What you must do is bring the corruption to the Jacks' attention, who will alert the whole community because they were unaware it was taking place right under their noses."

"Oh yes!" added Charlene. "We are aware of that fire in the woods. That is how we met Suzie."

Confidence continued, "The fire was purposefully set by a young boy hoping to get help for him and other children living in rescue cottages. They are there because of some form of trauma that occurred in their lives. Some of their parents have neglected or abandoned them in one way or the other and decided not to bring them back home, instead choosing to stay with their children's abusers. Other parents living with severe mental illnesses simply were not able to bring their children home. Some of the parents died and there were no other family members available to take in the children. Regardless of the circumstances, they need to be rescued from this particular home in the woods immediately.

"Oh yes!" barked Bliss and Charlene. "We are very familiar with those types of homes; we used to visit them with our past owners. The children loved us and were always excited to play with us."

"Unfortunately," Courage interjected, "their living environment is not meeting the criteria as required by the human authority that protects them. The owners collect money that is for the children's care, but in truth use very little toward their needs. The children are often fed foods that are full of fat because it is cheaper to buy; their clothing is always worn out or unfitted; their hair goes ungroomed causing many of them to be affected by hair lice. In addition, the children are often bitten in their sleep by bed bugs."

"Suzie," included Confidence, "since the fire, many of your family members have moved into the cottages making it unsafe for the children. Worst of all, Queenie, your cousins the Yellow Jackets have taken shelter on the outer perimeter of the cottage doors and the children's toys on the playground, making it dangerous for them to go in and out to play during the Spring and Summer."

"The owners also beat the children and as punishment, make them take care of their animals for shows. Sometimes they're even forced to sleep in the woods, but the staff calls it camp so as to not confuse the authorities. The owners continue to hire uneducated individuals who are insensitive, oblivious to the children's recovery needs, and who ultimately transfer their own anger onto the victims as well. Some of them have even been re-violated by employees," Courage disclosed.

"Even worse," revealed Confidence, "when the children go out in public, they are looked down upon and taunted by peers their age because of their shabby and unkempt appearances."

"Well did any of the workers report the problems they found to the authorities?" asked Mommy Nancy.

"Yes," said Courage. "Any good workers that have spoken up and addressed the issues were slowly but surely run off by the owners, leaving the children in an untenable position. Other workers were so intimidated that they stood by and did nothing, particularly because they had learned through various social events in the community that the Investigator assigned to the home is friends with the owners. The Moral Fiber Characters have always known this, but the Investigator's authority is unaware that the relationship has become unprofessional with the owners and that he's been ignoring their bad behaviors toward the children. As a result, the staff are intimidated and do not know who to trust at this point, given he is with the authorities. Even the children have attempted to report the maltreatment to other adults in the community by going as far as passing notes when out in public. Sadly, their pleas were ignored and some of the adults even reported the children to the owners, who in turn beat and punished them in retaliation. Other children reported incidents to their teachers, but unbeknownst to them, one of the owners is friends with the Principal of the school. These young ones are in a defenseless position everywhere they turn."

"That is awful!" droned Queenie. "How can humans be so unfeeling for each other? Have they lost their way?"

"It is obvious that they have," screeched Mommy Nancy, "because there is no other explanation. You and I met, fighting over our babies. What mother would abandon her babies before they are able to fend for themselves? It makes no sense! Boohoo, woo, boohoo, woo, woo," she cried. "Just awful; it breaks my heart. I want to burst out into a sad melancholy song."

"Yes, it is very awful," Courage agreed. "This is why we are reaching out to the critters. The community has been blinded by their own sight. On the surface, the owners look like noble citizens who are doing the public a splendid duty, keeping the children from wandering around and being wayward in the streets. The children are very confused on the Investigator's role, given they thought he was there to protect them. Now that they see him laughing and taking pictures at animal shows with the enemy, they no longer trust him. This is why Confidence is here to assist me with this mission because it is going to take great confidence from your superior intelligence to get the right humans involved to protect these children."

"At this point," added Confidence, "because of the neglect, losses, and many disappointments from their parents, caretakers, and now the investigator, some of the children have become very angry, untrusting and disillusioned. They have started to turn that anger outward, not only towards the adults but themselves as well, even trying to end their own young lives. Others are taking chances like running away from the environment, putting their lives in high risk situations to do so. The owners are very upset that they may lose money if the children do not calm down. Their remedy now is having the workers take them to a Physician in the community who places the children on medications hoping to control their behaviors."

"As you have already seen," said Courage, "the fire did lots of damage and the young soul that started it is now locked up in juvenile detention. We really need your help to protect the rest of the children before they self-destruct their young lives. This is why all of your abilities are critical to this assignment, which brings us to the moral fibers."

Moral Fibers
Character of Collaboration
"The first moral fiber you all will need is the character of Collaboration to focus and work in synchrony with each other while using your own

62

unique skills; otherwise, you will not be able to obtain the other three fibers you need to complete this assignment. The character of Collaboration is a very sensitive one who does not work alone. It only functions in a relationship, therefore the spirit of Communication works along its side. You will need to create a strong verbal alliance to get this task done, or the children will remain in the owners' care," Courage explained.

"Oh my," Pauli gasped. "Collaboration sounds so controlling, but we have already taken the initiative to work together when we saved Charlene."

"Yes you did," declared Confidence. "You are all well on your way, so it will be easy to exchange creative ideas to help rescue the children. This is where the strength of your teamwork is built."

Abilities
"The second moral fiber is simply to hone in on your natural abilities and skills that each of you were born with to survive. For example, Mommy Nancy you can fly, so your flight and singing skills are highly in order to oversee and communicate from above to the critters below. Suzie, your abilities to get in and out of small spaces, dig holes and move fast will be critical to this mission. Queenie, your flying skills as well as your ability to sting will be extremely necessary. Charlene you are still healing, but you will have a significant role in using your superior intelligence to channel key information to the Jacks and get their attention for the children. Bliss, you will carry messages between Charlene and the critters in the woods when the Bookers let you out in the mornings and evenings. Tamera will have your task ready for you each day and you will pass her information during those times."

Character of Resistance

"The Third fiber you will need is the character of Resistance; meaning you will need to resist any fears, barriers, thoughts or things including yourself that will delay or stop you from accomplishing this goal. I must forewarn you that this character is mean, challenging and will not back down until it recognizes your resiliency and determination."

"Oh no!" Suzie squealed very loudly. "My uncle has told many stories about the character of Resistance. We are all females, there is no way we can counterattack the things it will impose on us."

"In that case Suzie, go ahead and count yourself out," responded Confidence. "If you are going to use your female energy as an excuse to surrender to Resistance, then you will definitely hinder this assignment."

"No, that is not what I meant. I was just thinking of how tough it was for him and the other males in my family to deal with that character.

"Suzie, your family members are survivors. Remember what your uncle has taught you," Charlene chided.

"Suzie, have you decided if you are up for this task or not?" asked Confidence.

"Oh, but I am!" she replied.

"By the way, Pauli you will need to take the lead position during this mission."

"Why me?" Pauli posed. "I have not ventured far out into the woods, plus I am mostly domesticated. Why not Bliss? She has all of the confidence any critter would ever need."

"After the mission you will be able to answer your own question," countered Courage. "As far as Bliss, you will understand her more afterwards as well. Besides, you have a critical and extremely sensitive role to carry out with the children. By the time this is over, you will have just as much confidence if not more than Bliss."

Character of Endurance
"This brings me to the character of Endurance which is the fourth and final fiber; without it there is no rescuing of the children. It is just that simple. Now Endurance works with an energy named Integrity. Integrity, while very quiet, will challenge your reliability and steadfastness throughout this assignment. With this understood, although the children will be unaware that you are there to help, they will soon find solace with your presence and begin to heavily rely on you as an escape from their reality. With all of that said, it is now your choice if you will proceed," Courage concluded.

The Critters Accept the Assignment
"How can we not take the assignment after you have pulled on our nurturing heartstrings?" shrieked Mommy Nancy. "You knew exactly what you were doing. We are all mothers and there is no way that we could allow those children to stay in such a dilemma."

"Not only that," Charlene added, "you have also pulled on our own personal traumas and losses that align with the same reason the children were taken to the home. Now we have no other options but to feel morally compelled to act accordingly and do this, unless we are monstrous wolves ourselves. Just saying."

"Yes," replied Bliss. "This little diverse group has too much going on for me. I was just taking my afternoon walk, trying to blow out my mane when I heard all of this noise. I should have kept walking then, but no, I wanted my attention. Well now that I am here, I too have no choice but to join the critters and take on this assignment. When are we going to get started because I've got walks to take honey?"

"Ok," said Courage. "We take that as a 'Yes', you all are in agreement."

"Yes, yes," roared the critters.

"Well, may the Moral Fiber Characters be with you. Release the characters Confidence!!!!!" And off they vanished.

"Ugh," waffled Bliss, "I am exhausted hanging out with you ladies. I need a nap. Ooh Charlene, pooch is it always this much drama?"

"Starting to look that way," muttered Charlene. "I need a nap as well."

"If it is not one disaster, it is another," Suzie lamented. "When will it all end?"

"When we all return back to that good ole garden of peace," Queenie responded, "which I am so looking forward to this fall."

"What is this garden of peace?" asked Pauli.

"The one that we were all kicked out from along with the humans after a critter deceived them," answered Mommy Nancy. "I can hardly wait to get there myself."

"That is just an old critters' tale that has been passed down through time," Pauli retorted.

"Well maybe with your kind," droned Queenie. "But my kind still believes in the return to that great place where we will forever make glorious golden honey and never again endure the disasters of this wilderness. Of course, it is your will to believe as you please."

Mommy Nancy flew around the critters and whistled, "That's what is so wonderful about the yard; we all have free will to be persuaded as we choose. Whether we believe in tomorrow's garden of peace or not, today the children are in harm's way and we are the one yard right now where our differences are greater as one. Our oneness is boundless for the children, so I am going to take a flight over there and scope out the place. I will give an update tomorrow on our plan to help them."

Queenie added, "Well it looks as if I have lots of work cut out for my homegoing after all. This is going to be the biggest send-off celebration among the Dauber family yet!"

"What are you saying?" Pauli snapped. "What does this have to do with your send off?"

"Pauli, you will see," buzzed Queenie. "Let me say it like this, when I leave this fall, I am going out with a blast. For now I'm off to round up some other queens and my cousins, the yellow jackets, because I have a massive plan for them to put in action that could help us out."

Suddenly the shack's door opened and Bliss and the other critters dispersed. Mr. Jacks walked out to the back porch and said, "Hey, that looks likes the pooch the Bookers got from the kennel." He sat down next to Charlene who put her head in his lap. He rubbed her head and asked, "What's wrong girl? You look so sad as if you are carrying the world on your shoulders."

Charlene whimpered.

"Well," said Mr. Jacks, "it looks like a storm is coming. The wind has been blowing around the leaves out here."

The dog leaned in closer to her owner.

"Charlene, you cannot just sit here staring at those woods. You are going to have to get back out there sooner or later; just like that old pooch strutting over there, walking as if she does not have a care in the world. I guess I'm going to have to take you out into the woods soon for some walks."

CHAPTER 19
The Critters Go to Battle for the Children

Early the next morning, Charlene and Suzie could hear Tamera clanging underneath the shack obviously trying to get their attention. Simultaneously, they also heard Mommy Nancy bellowing out the critters' melody as well. They slowly arose and made their way to the east side of the screened in porch while being careful not to wake the Jacks.

Pauli eased toward the porch and muttered, "Really Nancy, even the roosters are not awake yet."

"Listen," Nancy cawed, "early bird, early worms. While the ground is still moist, we must get busy about our mission. Anyway, in the spirit of collaboration it would be best if we worked the assignment in teams of twos; the critters with the fewest things in common would be paired in order to best help the children. So I figured Pauli and Suzie should team up to handle the cottages. Suzie can go in and run her family out, then my family would have meals for days."

"Whoa, whoa, whoa!" squealed Suzie. "What is this? Use me to feed your family? I do not think so! This is about the children, not your family. Mommy Nancy, I am surprised at you and your attitude about this mission. Out of all of us, I would not have expected such an attitude."

"I rather like the plan myself," purred Pauli. "We all can benefit from this."

Charlene barked loudly to get the critters' attention.

By this time Bliss walked up with her mane flowing in the wind. "Are you critters at it already this early in the morning? I heard your squealing and squawking all the way at the Bookers' shack. Settle down already. Where is the spirit of collaboration? You heard Courage say the character of collaboration is sensitive, so let's not make her nervous."

"I think Nancy was just kidding to get some ideas going," buzzed Queenie. "Right, Nancy?"

"Well partly yes and no," she admitted. "I am going to have to put up strong resistance when Suzie runs her family out of those cottages, because they are mighty tasty little creatures."

"Oh that is just awful," cried Suzie.

"But it is the truth," Pauli goaded.

"Well," Charlene interposed, "one thing we learned from Courage and Confidence is that the character of Resistance will cause us to delay our mission if we do not resist such urges. We don't want anything to delay helping the children, right?" She sneered at the critters and woofed, "This conversation is doing just that!"

"With that notion, it is a great idea that Suzie and Pauli go into the cottage." Queenie explained that the children would just love on the cat. "In the meantime, I am bringing some old friends who will help me create a huge disturbance with the owners' animals."

"Are they going to hurt the animals?" Pauli inquired.

"My friends are old skilled queens who know winter is coming fast. By the time they get the job done, the owners will want the children off of their property and in a whole other community, never to return. That's what a queen does honey. I just need you and Suzie to do your part with the children while we do what we do."

"Suzie and Pauli, are you ready?" Mommy Nancy asked. "You have a long journey ahead of you to get to the cottages."

Pauli very hesitantly moved slowly toward the path and then walked off into the woods with Suzie. Mommy Nancy and Queenie flew above them singing and dancing while guiding them along. Bliss and Charlene stayed back on the porch and plotted about how they were going to get the humans involved.

Bliss Motivates Charlene for the Assignment
Charlene shared with Bliss how the whole assignment had her in the dumps, thinking about the way she left her pups to save herself. She yammered on that it was the hardest thing she ever had to do, not knowing if she would ever see them again or how they would survive.

Bliss reminded her that the pups were old enough to survive and had she not left, she may not have survived herself. "After all, those babies are living their life now hon," yapped Bliss, "and you need to live yours too now that you are free!"

"Somehow I still think I should have made the sacrifice and never left them, no matter the situation."

"Well it looks like you made the right choice after all," countered Bliss. "Now get up, stop acting like a rat and let's go for a walk in the yard."

"Don't do that. Suzie is my friend," scowled Charlene. "Leave her alone."

"Oh that's right. I heard you make a distinction of Suzie as your best friend when you introduced me to the critters. I thought we were besties."

"I thought I had lost you forever," snorted Charlene.

71

"If that is what you call a best friend," scoffed Bliss, "then do not consider me on that list. Friends don't let you hover in a corner in fear of life, while they natter and maw on and on about their calamity. That's called codependency. Wouldn't you say so yourself?"

"Oh my goodness," woofed Charlene, "you are starting to sound like Mr. Jacks."

"All I am saying is," Bliss continued, "there is no time to lie around and see life as one big disaster just because you had a devastating experience. Plus, we can't let the children see us like this once they are free from their own misfortune. Now get up and let's go rumble around in the yard so your legs will become strong enough to play with them. Life is about being off to the next adventure in the wild." Off they went.

"By the way Bliss, did you ever run across old Jake at any of the shows after I left?" inquired Charlene. "Did he ever ask about me?"

"Oh, it's the old sire Jake you miss uh? Ha, I knew it! I am not parting one bone on that," yapped Bliss. "You know the old saying, about 'a dog that brings a bone will carry a bone'. I've got nothing for ya!"

"All of these issues about the children got me thinking about how I always wanted my own yard with my own sire and litter, that's all," confessed Charlene.

"Well I wanted my own doggie shack but am happy to crash with the Bookers at theirs; at least no one is kicking and beating on me to make me posture for impressions," woofed Bliss. "I don't mind domesticated training, because there are great benefits from good owners and lots of affection. However, if humans have to beat us into a posture, at some point their intelligence should kick in and say 'This is unnatural for the animals'. It appears that some of them have limitations on their intelligence," Bliss concluded. "I just could not take it anymore and am too pretty for all of that abuse. They would have to put me down the next time, because I am going to tear into them if they hit me again. I have feelings too!"

"I wonder how the others are doing out in the woods," pondered Charlene.

"I am sure they are just fine," Bliss responded.

Pauli Meets a Wild Pig in the Woods
As Pauli and Suzie ran through the woods to get to the cottages, suddenly a wild pig appeared ahead of them, looking right at Pauli. She meowed very loudly as if she was hollering at Mommy Nancy for not warning her.

Suzie ordered, "Quick, climb the tree!"

Pauli froze and stared at the pig and the pig at her, "I can't, I can't climb the tree!" she cried back.

Mommy Nancy and Queenie suddenly swooped down and began swirling very fast around the pig's head several times to distract its attention.

Suzie kept squealing and going up and down the tree to show Pauli how to climb it. "Pauli resist your fear, resist your fear and resist your fear! Just leap Pauli, leap Pauli, like you own the tree! Leap Pauli, leap like you own the tree! Pauli, leap! Leap! Leap!"

Finally, the cat took a giant leap and kept going higher until she was far up in the tree. She caught hold of a nice thick branch but was shaking all over.

Suzie yelled, "Just hang onto the branch!" She then climbed up, took her tail and gently stroked Pauli's back to help calm her down. "There, there," she squeaked. "You are okay now. Open your eyes."

"I do not think so," she purred back.

"Yes you can," Suzie reassured. "Consider yourself wild now. Once you have met a wild pig and survived, you are a beast of the woods."

"Don't make me laugh. I do not want to fall off of this branch," replied Pauli. "By the way, thank you Suzie. You could have easily struck and hurt me in my vulnerability with your tail, but instead you used it to gently calm me down. Queenie, please sting that wild beast for me."

"No, no, no. Did you not hear what you just told Suzie? I tell you Pauli," Queenie snapped, "sometimes you come across like a double entendre. I am not wasting my stings on him. Between Mommy Nancy and I, our spirit of annoyance is good enough. That old beast does not want any more of our irritation and will soon leave."

Pauli Shares Her Vision
Mommy Nancy twittered and chirped, "Since the pig is forcing us to wait for his departure, we might as well use it as a signal to lock down our plan for Pauli once she arrives to the cottage."

"Yes, yes. I have been thinking of a scenario where I could very elegantly and gracefully walk like Bliss while carrying Suzie on my back," Pauli suggested.

"Because I know you, I know you are been sarcastic about Bliss; but I think it is a brilliant idea!" Queenie exclaimed. "The children will find it very fascinating and exciting. Suzie what do you think?"

"Although the vision may be just fine, I prefer better if I am asked to participate rather than it be assumed that I will automatically go along with everything. Just because we are hanging out here on this branch together does not mean we are no longer independent creatures. I still appreciate the opportunity to graciously accept or decline my own contributions. Besides all of that, I do not even get your full concept. What is the end result of this idea that I have been preselected to parade in?" questioned Suzie.

"I get it," piped in Mommy Nancy. "It's like a gift of excitement for the children, even if it is for only a moment. Oh yes, I can see them wanting this cat around."

"Thank you Nancy for getting my vision," responded Pauli. "This is why I tend to hold back my ideas, for fear of being rejected or unappreciated."

"Hold on," said Queenie. "Suzie didn't indicate that she did not appreciate it; she just prefers that you ask her to participate in your vision, which is what Courage and Confidence said. We have to communicate our creative ideas in a collaborative manner. By you putting your fears aside, we heard and like it. We still reserve our choice whether to participate in it and not feel controlled by your imagination."

"Since you put it like that, I've got so many raw talents. Let me share more with you!"

"No!" shrilled Nancy. "It's time to get down from this tree and head to the cottages before the children are home from school. It'll be the perfect time for them to see your vision in action."

"Get down? No way! I cannot climb down," roared Pauli.

"Listen here you little feline. You cannot stay up there hanging out on that branch forever. You and your fears are testing my patience. There is no fear in heights and I am getting hungry. The sun is making Suzie smell really good to me right about now and my resistance is very low. You have to get down or your friend will soon disappear," Nancy shrieked.

"Now wait, you greedy fowl! You need to take me off your menu if we are going to endure this assignment. Keep your mind on the children. You cannot keep threatening to devour me and my family every time your little hunger alert goes off. There are several bugs on those branches that can hold you over and I am sure your own family can drop you a meal or two in flight. Now pipe that out to them," Suzie angrily demanded.

"Oh my, my, my!" Queenie hissed and swirled. "Stopwith the name calling already. The spirit of resistance has reared its ugly head and I am reprimanding each one of you right now to stop it! Stop in the name of those motherless and fatherless children for whom the Moral Fiber Characters have reached out to us critters to help. Please, I beg of you now to control your urges!"

"I just need a little help going down," admitted Pauli. "I've been so domesticated that it has limited my natural ability to climb up and down trees, but I know I can do it."

"Yes you can," encouraged the wasp. "You were born to climb up and down trees, so no domestication can ever change that part of you. The children's situation has brought you back to your natural ability. It appears that the critter you have made as your enemy is the one that has so much in common with you. Watch how Suzie goes down and follow her."

"That's right. Just take it one mitt at a time like you own this tree, honey," the rat directed. "Come on now, I will help you and I trust that you won't eat me in the process of our descent."

"One mitt at a time," repeated Pauli. "I am turning down my fear and owning this tree. Thank you, Suzie. I would have never thought out of all the critters, that a little fury rodent like you would help me to overcome such a phobia."

Suzie led Pauli down the tree, while Queenie and Mommy Nancy quickly led them both to the back of the woods where the children lived.

Pauli and Suzie are Noticed by the Children
Mommy Nancy squawked very loudly that she could see the big yellow school bus with the children in it.

Pauli quickly put her vision into action and laid down for Suzie to climb onto her back. She remembered Bliss' elegant and graceful stride across the yard and began mimicking her walk along the rural road on the outer side of the woods. As the bus got closer, in her most stealthy catlike manner and tabby coat of fur, she calmly walked with Suzie standing mounted on her hind legs.

As the bus got closer, the children saw them and began screaming and yelling about the cat walking with a rat on its back. They were so excited and could hardly believe their eyes. They begged the driver to stop, but the driver only slowed down the bus. Pauli kept right on walking in the same direction as if she did not see them. The children were so thrilled and prayed the cat would come to their property. The driver arrived to the cottages and told them to ask the owners if they could have the cat. They just shook their heads because they had been told 'No' in the past whenever they asked for a pet. The children got off the bus and looked around for the amusing critters but both were gone.

Pauli and Suzie were hiding near the edge of the woods and saw a huge man standing on a porch who yelled, "Boys, go straight to the pantry and straighten it out! The rats have gotten into the food again. There will be no snacks until it is done."

One of the boys yelled back, "But I have to go to the bathroom!" Another shouted, "But I have homework to do or I am going to fail my class!"

"Thirty seconds in the restroom and then straight to the pantry!" the man screamed at them both.

A woman came hollering from around the corner, "Girls, get in line for your medications because we are not going to have any drama tonight. No drama! Are we clear?" It was the voice of Nurse Mad Lady, at least that is the name the girls had given her because she always seemed to be mad.

"Yes, ma'am," answered the girls.

Pauli and Suzie Enter into One of the Cottages
In the meantime, Queenie met up with her friends out on the property and Mommy Nancy went back to the shack. Suzie told Pauli she was very familiar with the property and knew an opening where they could

slip into one of the cottages. They had no idea what they were about to encroach upon. The inside turned out to be a huge cellar in one of the boys' cottages, which was set up for punishment. They saw one boy on his knees in the corner with his face to the wall. The critters sat very quietly behind storage and watched him for a long time to see what was going to happen next.

"At some point soon we will have to part," whispered Suzie, "but I will first search for food." As she poked around and got closer to the boy, she could see that he was crying then scurried back to tell Pauli.

By this time, the cellar door flung widely open and the huge man from the porch called for the boy to come out. He quickly shoveled in another boy and shouted, "You want a quiet place to do your homework? Here it is. Take all the time you need with the rats. And oh, don't forget your book Nay Nay!" He tossed a book at the boy.

Pauli and Suzie are Caught

"It's Nathaniel, you idiot," snarked the boy. He then reached over to grab the book and found himself face to face with Pauli and Suzie. Because the pair knew their purpose, they stood firm and stared right back hoping he would not run. In a quiet inquisitive manner the boy said, "Hey! What are you doing here? I'd recognize you two anywhere." He then leaned over, took one hand and gently rubbed the top of Pauli's head. He held out the other hand towards Suzie, who recognized his gesture as welcoming.

"I used to have a pet rat and a cat before my parents were killed in a car accident." Nathaniel was very small in stature for his age, twelve, and was often underestimated by staff. Little did they know that he had been writing notes and keeping dates regarding all of their bad behaviors toward him, his younger brother and the other children since the date of his arrival to the home. After petting the critters, making his notes and closing the book, he fell asleep. Nathaniel was abruptly awakened by clanging pipes in the cellar as water turned on and off above in the cottage for bath time. He realized it was now past supper time and knew that soon the next shift would come in. The man from earlier, Mike, would send him back into the cottage before they arrived, without a bath or dinner. The boy was hoping his favorite staff Bernita would be on duty tonight. Not only was she pretty, but she kind of reminded him of his mother.

He knew the routine so he motioned for his new pals to go back behind the storage and then he stood away from the door of the cellar out of sight. As expected, the door of the cellar abruptly swung open again and Mike threw down a pot of dirty dish water before pulling the light string on and off then walking away. Nathaniel waited until he heard the footsteps stop in their usual spot in the grass. He quickly ran up the cellar stairs and into the cottage as he passed Mike smoking off to the side of it.

After checking to see if Bernita had signed in, he realized that Mike was working the overnight shift as well today. He quickly grabbed two apples from the kitchen counter, hid them under his clothes and then dove into a sleeping bag on the floor in the living area with other boys. Unfortunately, they did not have beds because the owners purposely overfilled the cottages with children in order to make as much money as possible.

Nathaniel was aware that he had just enough time to give one of the apples to his little brother Henry, who also did not get dinner, before Mike returned to the cottage. Although he was still hungry, he would at least get a good breakfast at school the next morning. His only hope now was to get a good night's sleep. However, the chance of that happening was little to none between Mike talking to his friend who would stop by shortly, followed by loud snoring once his friend left.

Nathaniel Has a Secret
The next day as the children got on the bus for school, they were still excited and talking about the cat and rat phenomenon they had witnessed along the road the day before. Nathaniel made sure he sat next to Henry and quietly told him about his adventure in the cellar. He divulged a plan to get them in trouble so they would be sent down to the cellar after school today as well.

Holler Stone Creek
Later that evening after school, the brothers began horse fighting and goofing around, knowing it would irritate Mike. He grabbed them both but instead of throwing them down into the cellar, their plan backfired as he yelled for another staff member Tiffanie to haul them off to 'Holler Stone Creek'. The children gave the creek this name after hearing the echoes of their hollering bounce off of the stones that surrounded the loud gushing creek when the owners and staff were beating them.

Suzie had been spying on the inside of the cottages and kept Pauli up to date on the children's activities; so when she saw the boys being dragged off, she quickly scrambled down and they followed closely behind. The two critters could hardly believe what they witnessed. Pauli could tell that this was neither Nathaniel nor Henry's first time as they knew exactly what to do to shorten their beating.

Suzie began to cry, "Boohoo, boohoo, boohoo."

Pauli silently cried and hissed, "Come on, let's go. We have lots of work to do."

Disaster Among Us

Pauli and Suzie were so upset that they could hardly wait for Tamera to come so they could send a message back to the shack. They knew they had to get help fast and ran back to the cellar in 'mommy mode', because the staff was going to throw the boys down there next. Just as they predicted, the cellar door flew open and the boys were tossed inside. As soon as the door closed, Pauli hissed. She and Suzie immediately went over and began licking and comforting the boys who were very happy to see them. Nathaniel shouted, "I knew you would be here! I just knew it!" The children sobbed to the cat and rat as if they could understand their tears. Nathaniel muttered about how he was going to get revenge someday. He soothed Henry as best as he could while their critter friends continued to comfort both boys until they fell asleep. During this time, Pauli shared with Suzie a plan of action to help them. Soon the staff threw a dirty pan of dishwater down and the brothers jumped up and ran into the cottage.

CHAPTER 20
Mommy Pauli Takes Charge

Still in full blown Mommy mode, Pauli could not think about anything else except saving the children. She had just heard Tamera clanging around and rushed out along with Suzie to meet and bring her up to speed regarding their observations.

Tamera grunted, "So, it is far worse than what we had imagined. My family and I have always wondered about that echo because we knew it was not of any other critter. Oh how sad," she moaned. "I will make sure Bliss gets this message right away. We must save the children." Tamera rushed back through the woods to meet up with Bliss before she completed her evening walk.

Pauli and Suzie headed back to the cottages with a plan of action. The staff continued tossing child after child into the cellar, completely oblivious to the fact that they were being watched. While this was happening, Suzie solicited several of her family members to join her cause. They worked tirelessly and quietly trying to widen an opening far away in a very dark corner of the cellar; the plan being to guide the children through the hole, out into the woods and ultimately to the Jacks so that they could help them. For now, Pauli continued to comfort Nathaniel, Henry and others boys that they had let in on their secret.

Bliss Pleads With Charlene to Turn Down Her Fears
Meanwhile back at the shack, Bliss met with Charlene and told her about the children's beatings and how it was past time to put her fears behind and allow Mr. Jacks to walk her into the woods. She pleaded on the importance of getting him to Holler Stone Creek before the children's

83

spirits were totally broken. Charlene muttered that she would think about it overnight.

Charlene Contemplates Turning Down Her Pain

The news spread quickly to other critters who all got in mommy mode as well in preparation for the rescue mission. They had heard about Courage and Confidence's request to save the children, but did not have a clue as to the extent of what that really meant until they learned about the abuse. For Bliss and Charlene, it was all too familiar and too close for comfort. Now they finally had an opportunity to take a stand and do something about it, even if it meant helping another kind.

Charlene was nervous all night thinking about the wolves in the woods, but she knew she had to act. The thought of going out there brought a recurring nightmare of the wolves laughing at her pain. While struggling to rest, she was approached by Onyx, the Jacks' house cat.

He empathized with her apprehension about going back out to the same place where her attack occurred, but she had to for the children.

Charlene asked how he knew about them.

"I know everything that goes on around here. Just because I'm a house cat and stay to myself, doesn't mean I don't pay attention to details. I know you see the wolves stalking you in your sleep; I hear you moaning, growling and whining every night. I feel your pain Charlene," Onyx purred softly. "I even know about your friendship with Suzie. Although, I am not sure it is the best one for you, but it is what it is for you now anyway."

"Listen young Onyx, Suzie is very sweet and kind," defended Charlene. "What have you heard that would make you think such a thing?" For the entire time Charlene had been with the Jacks, she mostly kept her distance from Onyx and he from her. "I am surprised at your comments," she said, "since you have known about Suzie but never went after her; you usually chase anything you see!"

"It is obvious," Onyx replied, "that when any two critters of different kinds share one meat bone, they are friends; besides, you did not thump her away. All I am saying about Suzie, is that friends encourage friends to move forward and not stay stuck in their situations. It just seems as if she needs you to be sick, for herself. Anyway, fear is designed to make you move; those wolves just forced you to go deep down inside of yourself to feel the pain you were afraid to deal with. It is time for you to move forward from your past situation, but you're still laying here contemplating at a time when you are most needed. So now it's your turn to listen up Charlene. I know you have been very depressed about leaving your pups behind since coming here and then your cousins did what they did to hurt you. However, you have already survived their attack which puts you in an even better position to reach inside of yourself and put your power right where your doubt is. Going back out into the woods will give you strength and put you right where you need to be. I just hate to see you suffer so unnecessarily."

"Well, what about you Onyx? You are stuck here in the shack all day long," mumbled Charlene.

"I am just fine," he answered. "My service is to Mrs. Jacks. Her time is short as she is very ill."

"How do you know this?"

"You would know it as well, but you've been so preoccupied with all of your stuff that you haven't paid attention to what is happening around you," Onyx suggested.

"I am so sorry," Charlene apologized.

Charlene Ventures Out to the Woods

The next morning Charlene rose very early, headed straight to Mr. Jacks and bayed at him to let her out. He was surprised and rushed to grab one of his rifles from the gun cabinet. Henry yelled to his wife that he was taking their dog out for a walk. Mrs. Jacks hollered back to be careful out there and get back before lunchtime.

Just as they were entering the woods, Bliss came running and panting right into their path.

"Charlene, wait for me!" she yelped.

Mr. Jacks looked around and said, "Well look who's here Charlene. I guess Lady Bliss has decided to join us."

Bliss ran over, gave her pal a friendly rumble and then they all continued into the woods.

Pauli and Suzie Call for Reinforcements

Back at the cottages, Pauli and Suzie were becoming very frustrated down in the cellar because the door kept swinging open. The staff repeatedly tossed in so many different boys, that they were not able to get a decent sized hole dug. Deciding to venture out onto the property, the cat and rat found Queenie and her friends causing a ruckus amongst the show animals and their owners, who were running around shooing and swatting trying to avoid their stings.

The critters made sure to stay out of their way so that they did not get stung either. They motioned for Queenie to come over and quickly told her about the children's most recent beating and their dilemma of not being able to help them escape.

Queenie laughed about all the fun she and her crew were having and buzzed that it was time they put their final plan into action.

Pauli asked her what the plan was. The wasp quickly swirled back towards her friends and loudly hissed, "Queens, it is time to set the children free!"

"But wait, not now!" Pauli insisted. "There is a dark cloud coming up. Queens wait, hold on!"

It was all too late though, because they were off and headed to the cottages. All Pauli and Suzie could do was follow.

CHAPTER 21
Pandemonium, Mayhem and Revolution for the Children

"What did you expect? This is a human mission," fussed Queenie. "We are critters and the transformation that is about to take place is going to happen in critter time, not their time. The Characters knew just what they were doing when they selected us, going outside of the norm to get the humans' attention." Queenie then turned to her army, "I've got just one thing to say:

DO NOT hurt the little ones!

Pass the word throughout the formation.

Do Not hurt the little ones!!!

We are going in Nooooooow!!!" she buzzed.

The wasps flew in four groups and headed right toward their target. Coincidentally, the doors to two of the boys' cottages were wide open; the queens split up and dove inside each of them. From that point on, there was nothing but chaos, pandemonium and mayhem! The boys were all over the place.

Nathaniel and His Brother Escape

Nathaniel grabbed his notebook, his little brother Henry, two other boys and off through the woods they went. They were soon followed by Pauli and Suzie who took the lead to guide them. The boys ran as fast as they could to keep up with the cat. Soon they heard a voice screaming their names and tried to hide, but discovered it was right behind them. They realized that two of the girls, Yvonne and Trina, had escaped from their cottages when the staff was called to the boys' side for assistance. Nathaniel gave the command that they had better keep up because there was no turning back now.

The Children Get Stuck in the Woods

It was getting late in the afternoon, the children were hungry and then it started to rain. Their path became too wet and slippery to continue. Pauli saw a cave and led everyone there until the rain stopped. She and Suzie were nervous but determined to protect the children. They sent out signals for Mommy Nancy, hoping to get a message to Bliss. Since it was raining, it took her a while to find them but she eventually did and was updated on the mayhem created by Queenie and her friends.

As usual, being in good spirits, Nancy ensured that she would relay the information. She shared with them that during one of her flights earlier in the morning, she had seen Charlene and Bliss out walking with Mr. Jacks in the woods.

Mommy Nancy to the Rescue

Mommy Nancy flew back to the shack and squawked for Charlene who came to the porch. She was brought up to speed about what happened at the cottages and the children who escaped but were now stuck in a cave. Charlene asked Nancy to inform Bliss so they could go back out with Mr. Jacks.

Meanwhile, the rain let up and Pauli pushed for the children to move forward toward safety. It was getting dark and they were scared, crying and hungry, but Pauli was not giving up. She and Suzie were determined to get them all through the woods before nightfall. They knew the wolves and the wild pig would soon pick up on their scent and they could not stop now. The bigger boys started carrying the smaller children on their backs and everyone ran as fast as possible. Although slightly disoriented, the critters worked very closely as a team to recall their path. They heard the chirping of Mommy Nancy's family and knew they were getting closer to the shack. Daylight seemed to be fading faster than ever.

Unfortunately for Charlene, Mr. Jacks was nowhere to be found. She and Bliss were on their own and had to enter back into the woods alone. Charlene mustered up all of her courage and told Bliss that it was "now or never". They hauled off following Pauli and Suzie's scent and the sound of Nancy's overhead squawking. Soon she called out to both teams that they were approaching each other; by this time, they could also hear Queenie buzzing overhead with her friends.

The children heard the dogs' barking and became afraid, but Pauli kept pushing forward and sending body signals that everything was okay.

Nathaniel was very in tune with her, trusted her guidance and told the other children not to worry.

Trina screamed that she was afraid of dogs and Nathaniel promised that he would protect her; it seemed to calm her down and they continued.

Suzie, who was running faster than Pauli, alerted her that she had just seen Charlene and Bliss. They all soon met up and the cat allowed the dog to sniff her so the children would know they were safe.

Bliss took charge at that point to escort everyone the rest of the way to the shack. Nathaniel, who had seemingly become the 'Critter Whisperer', commanded the children to continue to follow and they obeyed him. The group made their way to the very edge of the woods, but abruptly stopped when they saw a man standing on a shack's porch talking with a Policeman. Suddenly, they heard the howls of wolves nearby. The children were terrified and Charlene shook with fear as the sounds got closer.

Then from out of nowhere, a loud clanging sound came ringing from behind the shack. Mr. Jacks laughed and said, "Oh, that's that opossum. She's been living around here for years."

The policeman laughed, got back in his vehicle and drove off.

Mr. Jacks looked up at the sky and could be heard saying it appeared it was going to rain again. He yelled for Charlene. She and Bliss both barked to let him know they were close by. He went back inside and they bayed for the children to follow them as the other critters ran to the edge of the shack.

CHAPTER 22
The Critters Collaborate: Final Plan of Rescue

Mommy Nancy was extremely wired and anxious to complete this mission. She told the critters that she had a final plan to get the Jacks back outside to see the children who were now crying, scared and upset. She reminded them of the time Mrs. Jacks broke up the fight between them and how they needed to replay that fight to get the Jacks' urgent attention. The critters quickly agreed.

At this moment, the children didn't know what to do nor understood what was going on, but they sensed that something unusual was about to happen as the critters were huddling together. Nathaniel, still in tune with nature, instructed for the children not to move.

Suddenly the critters all repositioned themselves and began making loud squawking, meowing, buzzing, barking, squealing and clanging sounds. It was so loud that both Mr. and Mrs. Jacks came running out of the shack immediately to see what was happening. There standing in front of them was Charlene, Bliss, Pauli, Nancy, Tamera, Suzie and the children.

Mrs. Jacks screamed, "My Lord! What are you kids doing out here? Where are your parents? Little girl, where are your shoes? Are you the children everyone is looking for? Get in here. Henry, call the police to come back right now!"

"Ma'am?" answered little Henry. "You want me to call the police?"

"No. I want Henry my husband, Mr. Jacks, to call the police."

"Ma'am, Ma'am, please! Please do not call the police yet," Nathaniel begged. "Please help us. We need help."

"Help you, what do you mean help you?" asked Mrs. Jack. "You are runaways from the Benson Children's Care Home."

"No ma'am. I mean yes ma'am, but there is a reason. Ma'am, Sir please hear us out," Nathaniel pleaded. "You see, there are bad things happening over there and no one is listening to us. Please, I have been taking notes about everything that goes on there. My daddy said that someday I am going to be a really good lawyer."

"Who is your daddy and where is he," Mrs. Jacks inquired.

"My parents were killed over in Jackson County last year and we got sent to the Benson Children's Care Home because we had no other family who could take care of us. My uncle is in the military and told us that when he gets out, he is going to come and get us; but we have not heard from him since our parents were buried," explained Nathaniel.

"Well you children calm down and sit down," said Mr. Jacks. "Here are some towels to dry yourselves. Penelope, please get them something to eat, they look mighty hungry there. What is your name young man? You seem to be the leader of this crew."

"It is Nathaniel."

"Do you mind letting me see that notebook of yours?"

"No sir, but it is mine," the boy declared.

"Sure, I will give it back to you," promised Mr. Jacks. "Oh my, mmn. This is pretty impressive note taking here. Now are you claiming these things happened at the Care Home since your arrival there? Or is this hearsay from other children?" he probed.

"If it is in red ink, then it either happened to me or I witnessed it myself," Nathaniel responded. "If it is in blue ink, then I heard it when I was in another room. If it is in green ink, the other children talked about it on the bus. You see, the bus is the only private place where we can share our pain. We are family there."

"Looks like your red ink outweighs the other ink, with the green ink running close behind," said Mr. Jacks. "If all of these things are true, then it appears we have a bit of trouble on our hands here in the community. Wouldn't you say so?"

"I say so," agreed Nathaniel. "One time the staff took my notebook and I thought I would never see it again, but another kid got in trouble around the same time and was taken to Holler Stone Creek. While they were out, I grabbed it and replaced it with my school notebook."

"Well it sure sounds like you have angels around protecting you and your notebook young man; but there is one thing I want to see for myself, and that is Holler Stone Creek," insisted Mr. Jacks.

"No! PLEASE do not make me go back there!" cried Nathaniel.

"No, I would not make you go back. My dog Charlene here and I will find it on our walk tomorrow," he replied.

Suddenly there was a loud knock at the door. Mr. Jacks went to check it and it was the same Policeman from earlier. He told Henry that they saw children's footprints near the edge of the woods and asked if he had heard anything. The children were very nervous and Mr. Jacks was still holding Nathaniel's notes in his hand.

He hesitated, but then told the Officer that he and his wife were preparing to turn down for bed and would alert the authorities if any children knocked on their door after he left. The Policeman went about his way to continue the search while the couple fed the children and prepared them a place to sleep for the night.

CHAPTER 23
The Community is Made Aware of a Crime

Very early the next morning, Mr. Jacks arose and went out into the woods with Charlene, Bliss, his rifle and a camera. The canines picked up on Pauli and Suzie's scent from the previous day and soon found the creek. Just as they were approaching, Mr. Jacks saw a staff member from the Benson Children's Care Home dragging a child to one of the stones, so he pulled out his camera and began taking pictures. Charlene and Bliss could not bear to watch and simultaneously ran and attacked the staff who took off after being bitten.

The child was left at the stone. Mr. Jacks went over and introduced himself, then asked the boy to come to the shack with him. The child, Beau, agreed once he heard that Nathaniel and the other children were there.

Mr. Jacks returned home with Beau, called his brother-in-law who happened to be a lawyer and told him about the children's plight. Marquis Hawkins came over right away and took each of the children's statements. He asked Nathaniel if he could borrow his notebook and make copies. Nathaniel agreed but did not want to depart with it yet.

Mr. Hawkins then called Children's Protective Services and reported the children's story. He instructed Henry and Penelope to take them all to the local emergency room to be checked out by a Physician. Next, the Attorney called the Police department and requested an Officer meet him there to take a report; but he also called a local News Reporter to expose what he had learned before the Bensons got a chance to tell their story. He made up in his mind that they would have their day in court.

As the children were getting into the Jacks' car, it was around noon and all of the critters were huddling together on the side of the shack looking on. Nathaniel and little Henry ran over to Pauli and gave her hugs. They saw Suzie hovering in the corner of the shack and gently patted her on the head before quickly running back to the car.

Bliss gushed, "Oh so sweet. Good job Pauli and Suzie. You really bonded with them!"

"Well, we have completed our mission," buzzed Queenie. "We are an awesome team."

"Yes we are," purred Pauli.

"That we are," squealed Suzie. "Who would have ever thought?"

"Courage and Confidence," woofed Charlene.

The critters burst out laughing in accomplishment.

As Mr. Jacks finished loading the children into the car, News Reporters soon surrounded them, but he quickly pulled off. The reporters then went over to Attorney Hawkins and began talking to him.

CHAPTER 24
Critters Get a Visit from Courage and Confidence

As the critters watched the human commotion, suddenly a swirl of leaves and familiar coughing sounds came up in their midst. "Here we meet again in the midst of your self-adulating and you are not even done yet," stated Courage.

"But the children have been rescued!" proclaimed Suzie.

"This is only the beginning of your mission. Remember, endurance is the final step," added Confidence.

Queenie whined, "What is possibly left that we still need to do?"

Charlene suggested, "What if we honor them for their bravery, courage and confidence for having to endure such horrific mistreatment as young souls?"

Mommy Nancy chirruped, "That is the best idea yet! One way we could do that is to rid the echo of children hollering at that Holler Stone Creek by creating new sounds there."

"Yes, yes!" agreed Courage and Confidence in unison. "Now that is a selfless act. Do not forget to involve the humans."

"That is easy to do," Mommy Nancy declared. She whispered to the team a plan on how they could do just that and the critters agreed.

Later that night, the Jacks returned home. While having tea and watching the news, they saw that the remaining children had been removed from the Benson Children's Care Home and taken to the local hospital for medical evaluations as well. The owners and several staff were finally under investigation for child abuse and other legal issues pertaining to the waste and abuse of government funding. All of the Children would be placed in reputable Care homes with closer supervision by Children's Protective Services.

CHAPTER 25
The Children Are Honored

Over the next few days, the critters were up bright and early even before Tamera turned in to rest. They all joined in together with their voices and created a new sound along with Mommy Nancy's family. The sound was so unusual that it woke the Jacks up each morning like clockwork. They would go out onto their front porch, lean over the rail, and listen to the various ranges coming from each critter, completely amazed by the sounds of nature.

One morning Mr. Jacks said to his wife, "Penelope, this is the most beautiful sound I have ever heard in my life! You know, I believe those children and this gives me a great idea for them. I know you are not well these days but you are not done yet, my dear. We have work to do." He told her his plan for the community to come together and honor the children for their suffering that took place right under their noses.

"Oh Henry, that is a wonderful idea!" she concurred.

They began making several phone calls around the town including to local authorities regarding how to remove the saga of Benson Children's Care Home and Holler Stone Creek. Everyone wanted to return to the once safe community that they all grew up in. After all, the owners were not even from the area.

A few days later ideas began to flow in, including from Attorney Hawkins who informed the Jacks that this was not the first time the Bensons had been in trouble with Children's Protective Services. They were previously shut down in two other states for the exact same allegations. The property where the cottages were located belonged to the Leander family who made the Bensons leave immediately; they were not allowed to return. The Leanders wanted to donate the property, including the creek, to the community for use by the children.

Mr. Jacks agreed, "Then it shall be a huge park for the children where now the echoes bouncing around the creek will be the harmonious sounds of children running and playing." He came out of retirement to make sure it was done.

The Critters' Final Meeting of the Minds
By Fall, Inner Harmony Park had been developed and Holler Stone Creek was now named Golden Honey Creek.

The investigation was over. The Bensons and their staff were arrested and prosecuted.

Bliss, Nathaniel and his brother Henry were adopted by the Bookers.

Pauli was back in the house with the Jacks, Charlene and Onyx.

Suzie loved being back out in the woods with her family and was chosen as their new leader to guide them to a new field.

Tamera was still clanging around every night.

Mommy Nancy continued to make beautiful songs as she prepared for her winter migration.

Queenie introduced the new queen Lady Love and then prepared for her last flight along with friends to the garden of peace.

The group met for their final Meeting of the Minds but they were not alone. Once again those twirling twisting leaves rose up, along with a hoarse cough, as Courage and Confidence made their final entrance in the midst of the critters. This time no one was giving adulations to each other, they were instead very quiet. The Characters were also initially very quiet.

"Thank you for caring. Thank you all for having enough confidence in each other to collaborate your unique abilities, resist your fears and overcome barriers. Thank you for enduring each other's differences for the cause of rescuing the children," Confidence commended. "Without your courage to do so, they would not be free now. On behalf of all the Moral Fiber Characters, you are more than conquerors."

Courage nodded his head and said, "Thank you so much." Then as quickly as they appeared, they vanished.

Pauli mewed, "Is that it?"

Bliss winked and replied, "That is it. What else were you expecting?"

The End